Learn to Ride

with

The British Horse Society

Learn to Ride

with
The British Horse Society

Islay Auty FBHS

KENILWORTH PRESS

First published in 2003 by
Kenilworth Press Ltd
Addington
Buckingham
MK18 2JR

British Library Cataloguing in Publication Data
A catalogue record for this book is available from the British Library.

ISBN 0-872119-61-1

Designed by Paul Saunders
Layout by Kenilworth Press

Printed in Singapore by Stamford Press

Photo credits
All photos are by **Trevor Meeks**, except the following:

Bob Langrish 2, 15, 52, 64, 75, 93, 104 (both), 105 (both), 113, 116, 117, 118 (both), 119, 121 (both), 122
Steven Sparks 89
David Fraser 120
Steve Bardens 71 (top)
Linda Benedik 67 – reproduced by kind permission, from **Yoga for Equestrians**, by Linda Benedik and Veronica Wirth, published by Kenilworth Press (UK) and Trafalgar Square Publishing (USA)

Illustration credits
All drawings and diagrams are by **Dianne Breeze**, except the one on page 114, which is by Michael J. Stevens.

FRONTISPIECE: The pleasure of riding. A group enjoying the countryside on horseback.

Contents

Preface

This book is your gateway to learning to ride. If you are a new or would-be rider, looking for a clear and encouraging text to get you off to a good start, stimulate your interest and provide straightforward information on riding theory and lesson content, then this book is for you.

Using simple explanations, assisted by diagrams and photos, it will help you as a beginner or novice rider to understand your early riding lessons and get more from them. It will enhance and reinforce the information you receive from your instructor(s) and will motivate you to seek further knowledge in whatever way you choose.

ISLAY AUTY FBHS, BA

Acknowledgements

The author and publishers are particularly grateful to the proprietor, staff, riders and horses of Gartmore Riding School (Hammerwich, Staffordshire) for their help in the preparation of this book. Individually they are: (Gartmore staff) Sam Bowyer, Joanne Moore, Andrew Hardisty, Catherine Bishop, Suzie Richards, Louise McKeown, Nick Lakin; (adults) Jackie Robinson, Susan Ryder, Karen Pearson, Tracy Guest, Teresa Watt, Julie Cooper, Sara Spires, Amanda Chatfield, Debbie Watson, Anne-Marie Goode, Trudi Graham; (children) James Francis, Julia Hardisty, Stephanie Spires, Francesca Evans, Parsley Newlands, Sam Pountney, Hannah Sadler, Sophie Hamilton. Proprietor Tracy Evans deserves a special mention.

Thanks are also due to Pat Shepherd, Steve Kenworthy, Carol Lyon and all at Croft End Equestrian Centre (Oldham, Lancashire); and to the Talland School of Equitation (Cirencester, Gloucestershire).

Photographers Trevor Meeks and Bob Langrish must be thanked especially for supplying such superb photographs. Likewise, Dianne Breeze for her artistic talent in producing such excellent illustrations.

Foreword

I am pleased to recommend this new title to you, a timely book from a popular author, Islay Auty. Many adults are now taking up riding. Within the BHS we attract new members who are mums with children starting school, professional men in their thirties who are keen to tackle a new sport, and older adults who have taken early retirement!

As their competence develops, pupils can take either the Society's Progressive Riding Tests or Junior Achiever Tests – a very popular way of learning to ride and acquiring an impressive collection of badges and certificates! More mainstream and special schools now offer riding at a local BHS riding school as an option within their physical education classes, which is opening up the sport and bringing a taste of the fun to be had from riding and caring for horses and ponies.

The BHS guards its reputation for high-quality training with great care. Remember that selecting a BHS-Approved riding and training centre for your tuition ensures that you are learning from trained instructors in stables where standards of horse care and horsemanship are high, and where your safety is assured. The BHS Quality Assurance inspections operate across the globe – so go for the best wherever you live!

I hope you find this book informative – and do enjoy your riding!

KAY DRIVER
Chief Executive, The British Horse Society

chapter 1

So you want to ride?

Introduction

There may be many reasons why you want to give riding a try:

- You may always have wanted to ride but never had the opportunity. While many sports need to be undertaken at a young age (e.g. athletics and team ball games), riding can be started at any age. Some new riders take up the sport on their retirement, when they suddenly find they have the time and the money to indulge themselves in something they have always wanted to do.

- You love horses; everything about them appeals to you – their beauty, their strength combined with gentleness, their soft, velvety muzzles, their grace and agility when galloping and jumping, their power. It follows that you want to be around them and ride them.

- You have a friend or sibling who rides. You have seen them riding and are very tempted 'to have a go'.

- You rode as a child, then all sorts of other things got in the way (e.g. boyfriends/girlfriends, exams, college, lack of funds, marriage, children, etc.). You now have some disposable income, more time and want to 'get back to it'.

True or false?

If you are contemplating taking up riding, here are a few of the things you will probably be told about the sport (usually from people who don't ride). Some of them are partly true, others totally false, but an involvement with horses can be wonderful in so many ways that the disadvantages are seriously outweighed.

- **It's an expensive sport.** True, but you can regulate how much you become involved, and one riding lesson per week will cost somewhere between £15 and £20 depending on where you live. Diving, gliding, parachuting and other stimulating activities can be as costly, or more so.

THE HORSE

Some of the qualities we admire in the horse are beautifully expressed in Ronald Duncan's 'Tribute to the Horse', which traditionally is read each year at the conclusion of the Horse of the Year Show:

'Where in this world can man find nobility without pride, friendship without envy, beauty without vanity?

'Here, where grace is laced with muscle, and strength by gentleness confined.

'He serves without servility; he has fought without enmity.

'There is nothing so powerful, nothing less violent; there is nothing so quick, nothing more patient. England's past has been borne on his back.

'All our history is his industry: we are his heirs, he is our inheritance.

'Ladies and gentlemen: The Horse!'

- **The horse is a dangerous creature – he bites at one end, kicks at the other and is uncomfortable in the middle!** Absolutely **not** true. Horses are not aggressive animals; if they bite it is because they are not happy, so if you are riding at a school where there are several horses that bite then find another establishment. Happy, contented horses rarely bite people; similarly they rarely kick unless you take them by surprise, in which case they may lash out in defence. Occasionally horses bite or kick each other, particularly in a close situation in a field (for example, if a group is waiting to be fed or to come in from the field they may resort to their natural methods of asserting a 'pecking order'). Avoid being in the way whenever there is a group of horses loose in this sort of situation, because then you might risk being kicked. If horses are handled firmly and with knowledge and consistency, they will rarely, if ever, bite or kick you. If you are well introduced to riding and competently taught, then any discomfort you may feel through unfamiliarity in the saddle should be minimal and will soon pass.

- **You will get cold, wet and muddy.** Maybe you will in winter, but these days there is such a good range of specialist clothing available to protect you against the elements while carrying out your new sport, that your discomfort will be minimal. Walking, fishing, football and rugby can be just as uncomfortable.

Talking the talk

Inevitably, as with anything new, riding will introduce you to a whole range of new terms and experiences. If you don't understand a new term, don't be afraid to ask what it means and what relevance it has to what you are doing or trying to do.

Here are a few basic terms that might help you at the beginning:

- **Riding school/centre / equestrian centre**. The name for a business that offers riding instruction to the general public. The riding school may also refer to the actual area in which you will have your riding lessons (see also manège / riding school / outdoor or indoor arena – below).

- **Horses**. Usually equines over 148cm high (14.2hh), which are used for adult riders and taller children.

- **Ponies**. Small equines up to 148cm high (14.2hh). While they look physically like small horses, ponies often behave with much more hardiness, canniness and individuality, which may originate from their native, often moorland, breeding.

- **Manège / riding school /outdoor** or **indoor arena**. This is the specific area where most formal riding lessons take place. The arena will usually be either 20m wide by 40m long, or 20m wide x 60m long, which are the sizes designated for dressage competitions. Some arenas are even bigger, allowing for more scope with class lessons where there are a larger number of riders in the group.

The stable yard ... with several interested and happy faces looking on.

A group lesson, in a safe, enclosed, all-weather-surfaced manège.

- **Markers**. Around the riding arena there will be letters, usually black on white. The standard markers – **A F B M C H E K** – are placed around a 20m x 40m school; there are additional markers (**P V R S**) in a 20m x 60m school. The letter **X** is nominally in the centre. These markers are used as reference points to help you move around the arena, change direction and ride school figures (shapes).

- **School figures**. Circles, turns, loops, serpentines and inclines are just some of the figures (or shapes) that can be ridden in an arena in all three gaits (walk, trot and canter).

- **Hacking**. The term used for riding out of the school into farmland, moorland or the surrounding countryside.

- **Tack**. The equipment that a horse wears, especially when he is ridden – e.g. saddle and bridle.

As your riding experience develops, so will your equine vocabulary. You will develop a range of specialist 'speak', which will give you an identity with other 'horsey' people.

So how do you begin?

If you have ever have sat on a horse/pony belonging to a friend, or on the beach on holiday, or on a trail ride or trek in the UK or abroad, this will have given you a brief idea of what it is like to sit astride a living animal with little or no idea of how to control it. These encounters can be scary, so if you want to move on to the next stage, you will need to get some proper tuition. The most usual way to do that is to find yourself a good riding school.

Licensed riding schools

In Britain all riding schools offering horse riding in return for payment are required, by law, to hold a local authority licence under the 'Riding Establishments Act'.

It is possible to obtain a list of these licensed establishments from the Environmental Health Department of your local or county council. It is then advisable to visit a riding school close to home and see what it has to offer.

If you are not familiar with riding and the horse world, it is easy to be 'blinded by science' or impressed by grand facilities (e.g. buildings, yard, house, vehicles); and your lack of knowledge of the sport means that you are unable to assess the standard of the horses or teaching that might be on offer in the school. So, if possible, take a 'horsey' friend with you, someone with sound knowledge of good riding practice. If you don't know anyone horsey, the following points should help you to ask the right questions and not be 'taken for a ride'.

British Horse Society Approvals scheme

Ideally, once a school is licensed by the local authority it should seek British Horse Society Approval. This requires the establishment to undergo a thorough inspection of its facilities, its horses and the standard of instruction that it offers, to meet strict criteria laid down by the British Horse Society. After an initial inspection which is pre-arranged, annual inspections are made unannounced and the Approved centre is obliged to uphold the standards expected by the BHS: to endeavour to offer to the riding public a service of recommend-

A group lesson at a higher level – note that the horse in the foreground is wearing a double bridle and its rider has a deeper (more advanced) riding position.

A well-organised office, offering a welcoming reception area for clients arriving to ride.

able and acceptable quality. BHS-Approved riding schools will have at least one member of staff on the payroll who holds a teaching qualification offered by the BHS. The BHS is the governing body in Great Britain, recognised by UK Sport for its instructor qualifications. Instructors holding a British Horse Society certification will have followed formal training and taken an examination in their teaching skills of riders at varying levels, from beginner to advanced (depending on the level of certification), both on the flat and jumping.

Your first visit to a riding school

On arrival at the riding school:

- Does anyone greet you as you enter the yard and ask you if they can help?

- If no one is around, is it clear where the reception or office is?

- Is the yard tidy, workmanlike, 'alive' and attractive?

If the answer to all the above is 'yes', the school will probably have a tidy, well-maintained yard, with flowers, hanging baskets or similar, some activity of people in the yard, horses' heads peering over stable doors, and generally some feeling of animation.

If the answer to the questions is 'no', the school will probably have an untidy, ill-kept yard, with peeling paint, generally poor maintenance, weeds, and an air of neglect. More than likely there will be no sense of activity or involvement, nor any interest in your existence.

If the school is BHS-Approved then (usually near the entrance of the yard or next to the office) there will be a blue plaque to indicate this.

THE BRITISH
HORSE SOCIETY
**APPROVED
RIDING
ESTABLISHMENT**
2003

If your first impression of the riding school is favourable and you are approached by a member of staff, ask if it is convenient for you to be shown around.

A well-run riding school should always welcome new clients. While it is easier for the centre if you are shown round by prior appointment, it is nevertheless good business practice to welcome visitors and show them around whenever they choose to come to the school, even if only by a junior member of staff.

WHAT TO ASK

- Who teaches the lessons? Do they have a BHS qualification?

- How are beginner rides taught? Individually? In groups? On the lunge? On the lead rein?

- How long will I be led/lunged?

- How big are the class lessons?

- Where do the lessons take place? In an indoor school? Outside in an all-weather arena?

- When do the lessons take place? Weekends? Evenings?

- How often are there lessons of my standard?

- What clothes should I wear? Do I need to buy anything special?

At the end of your first visit, you should feel like a welcome visitor, stimulated by what you have seen, especially if you have been able to stroke a few horses and see some lessons going on. You should feel eager to get started. You should want to:

- book your first lesson there and then;

- get home to see what clothes you can organise to wear for your first lesson;

- tell your friends the good news that you are going to learn to ride;

- count the hours until your first lesson.

On the other hand, if, after your visit, you feel:

- nervous about the environment or anything you have seen, especially the horses;

- not made to feel welcome, or even intimidated, by those you met in the school;

- uncomfortable about any aspect of the riding school, however minor;

then you must go and find somewhere where you do feel comfortable.

Either:

- Ring the British Horse Society (tel: 01926 707700) and ask for an up-to-date list of BHS-Approved riding schools in your area.

- Look in the *Yellow Pages* to see which riding schools are listed in your area as being licensed, and preferably BHS-Approved.

- Visit more schools until you find one you like.

Getting started

chapter 2

Booking your first lesson

You've decided to take the plunge: you are ready to book your first riding lesson.

If you can, call in again in person; otherwise make a booking on the phone. This second visit should confirm all the good feelings you had about the establishment on your first – that it was welcoming and eager to offer you a service.

The booking should be made in the office. Many centres have a daily diary, and some schools now make computerised bookings. There may be specific times for beginner riders' lessons, but there should also be some flexibility to offer you a lesson-time that will suit your commitments.

If you work full time then you may need lessons in the evenings or at weekends. If you have a part-time job or do shift work, you may want a lesson during a weekday. Many riding schools operate a six-day week, with Monday as their rest day. Some schools offer evening lessons on four or five days during the week, but give lessons only during the day at weekends.

When you first book your lesson, information should be taken about your height and weight. If you are booking by phone, please be honest about these matters. The staff need to select a horse that will be appropriate for your build. You must be truthful about your weight especially, otherwise the horse will inevitably suffer.

Your booking will be probably for a 30- or 45-minute session. You should be informed of the exact cost of the lesson (this may include VAT if it is a large commercial establishment). You should also be told what clothing to wear and whether you can purchase or borrow an approved riding hat.

There may be a rule whereby bookings must be cancelled up to 24 hours before the time or a charge of 50% or more will be incurred. A full charge may be expected if you just do not turn up with no reason given. Non-attendance causes serious inconvenience to a centre as the horse will have been prepared (i.e. groomed and tacked up) for you.

What to expect

At all times in a British Horse Society Approved riding establishment you should expect the highest standards of courtesy and attention. Politeness costs nothing and should be reciprocal.

The horses

The horses that you ride should look healthy and be well turned out. Look out for the following:

- The horses should appear cheerful (alert, ears generally forward and calm).

- The horses should be clean. If living in a stable, they should not have bedding in their manes or tails; they should be groomed with no stable stains, and their manes well maintained (pulled to a tidy length according to their type).

- The horses should have gleaming, shiny coats and well-fleshed bodies. You should not be able to count their ribs but neither should they be grossly over-weight.

- If living at grass, the horses may have longer coats and a shaggier appearance (particularly ponies in winter).

- Horses/ponies living at grass should still be well turned out for riders. They should have any mud brushed off and efforts made to present a tidy animal.

Your instructors

The number of instructors in a riding school will depend on the size of the establishment. Smaller riding schools may have only one qualified instructor and employ part-time instructors when they need them on busier days, such as

LEFT A casual stance from an uninvolved teacher – mobile phone in hand contributes to the lack of professionalism. **RIGHT** A workmanlike, tidy presentation, conveying a professional and involved interest in her rider(s).

weekends. It is advisable to be taught to ride by a person who has been trained specifically for the job. Ideally that person should hold a BHS qualification and be on the Register of Instructors. There are countless individuals throughout the country with vast personal experience of riding, but this does not automatically give them the know-how to pass that ability to someone with no experience. Some good riders also make good teachers, but not always. If you choose an instructor with a recognised teaching qualification you are more likely to make structured progress in your riding. Registered instructors have to abide by a formal code of conduct; they also carry public liability insurance for up to £10 million.

If you start your lessons in one of the bigger riding schools then there may be several different instructors of varying levels of expertise on the staff. Often the more junior members of staff take novice lessons under the (regular) supervision of senior staff. If you want one-to-one/private lessons with a more senior member of staff, this will probably be possible, but obviously the cost will be greater. Usually if you have a lesson with a more senior instructor it can boost your progress because of the superior ability of that teacher. Recognise, though, that there are benefits from working in a group situation, where riders learn from one another and at a slightly steadier pace than the intensity demanded by a one-to-one session. You may also find that you can be taught by different instructors if you do not keep to a regular 'slot' on a weekly basis. In a well-run school there should be some system for continuity in lessons if clients often ride with different instructors.

Getting the most from your lessons

The most important criteria, however, when you are receiving riding lessons are that:

- You enjoy the experience.

- You feel confident about the person who is teaching you.

- You feel comfortable about asking questions if something is not clear.

- Everything is clearly explained and progress is made according to your confidence and ability (i.e. you are not pushed into doing something you do not feel happy about).

- You look forward to your ride.

- You like the person teaching you – he or she is approachable and friendly.

- You like the horse(s) you are given to ride. As time progresses and you ride different horses, you will like some better than others, because some are easier to ride than others. However, you should never have to ride unsuitable horses that frighten you because they are ill-mannered and/or aggressive, e.g. laying their ears back and snapping their teeth.

Your first lesson - lunge or lead rein?

During your first riding lesson your horse should be under the direct control of your instructor or a competent 'leader' at all times.

First lessons are generally given either on the **lunge rein,** or on a **lead rein**.

Lunge lessons

Lungeing is the term used when a horse is controlled on a large circle (of between 15m and 20m diameter) by a long rein connected to the horse's tack and held by the instructor. In this situation the handler (lunger) can at the same time control the horse and teach the rider, who sits as a passenger on the horse's back. The horse works in a regular rhythm in walk, trot and sometimes canter, and the rider can concentrate on developing his skill without having to worry about the control of the horse.

Lunge lessons have the following **advantages**:

- The rider is free to concentrate on himself, especially his position and balance.
- The rider can be introduced to the gaits and the sensations of riding, while the horse remains totally under the instructor's control.
- They allow the rider to develop a sense of confidence in feeling the horse's movement – and in the instructor – by providing a safe environment.
- The instructor can clearly observe the rider at all times.

A moment's discussion during a lunge lesson.

The instructor's involvement and enthusiasm helps to maintain this young pupil's interest and concentration.

- The instructor can establish a good rapport through body language and positioning in the circle, with both the horse and the rider.

The **disadvantages** may be listed as:

- Some riders do not feel confident about having the instructor at a 'remote' distance, i.e. at the end of a long rein.

- The rider may develop small faults on the 'outside' of his body and these are not visible to the instructor from his position in the middle of the circle.

- If the horse is unsettled for any reason it may frighten the beginner rider before the instructor can bring the situation under control.

- A large amount of space is required for a 'one-to-one' lunge lesson, whereas several beginner riders could be taught together in a lesson taken by a competent instructor and several able leaders.

- Lunge lessons are labour-intensive on instructors, and physically demanding on horses.

Lead-rein lessons

Lead-rein lessons involve teaching the beginner rider with the control of the horse being taken by a leader. The leader may be the instructor himself, or a competent handler who leads the horse while the instructor teaches (usually more than one rider) from the centre of the arena.

The **advantages** of using this system for teaching beginners are:

■ Some riders, particularly children or those of a more nervous disposition, feel more confident because of the close proximity of the handler.

■ There is minimal risk of a horse becoming unsettled because the handler can deal with any such situation much more swiftly than when lungeing.

■ A group of riders can effectively be taught together with one instructor and several leaders. In this situation riders can learn from each other and share their enjoyment and problems.

■ Lead-rein lessons are less demanding on school riding space than lunge lessons.

The **disadvantages** are:

■ Some adults do not feel independent enough and want the 'freedom' offered by a lunge lesson.

■ Some riders prefer one-to-one teaching, in which case an individual lead-rein or lunge lesson might be more appropriate.

■ If the instructor is also the leader, his view of the rider is limited because he has to stay close to the horse's head.

Ultimately your choice of lunge or lead-rein lesson will probably be governed by:

■ What 'your' riding school offers.

■ What you feel will suit your needs best.

If 'your' school offers both, then perhaps watch both before making your decision. Or, be prepared to try both so that you know the difference and can make a more informed choice. If you are not sure, take advice from the instructor at the school. Bear in mind too that, generally, lunge lessons are more expensive than lead-rein lessons.

What to wear

You should be given clear advice about suitable clothing for riding. The following guidelines should help you choose what to wear.

■ You must be warm. If the weather is cold or wet and you will be riding outside, wear several light layers. These will keep you warm but will not be bulky and restrict your movement.

■ A waterproof jacket is essential if it is wet and you are riding outside, but this should be carefully chosen. Ideally the slightly longer than waist-length coats which do up down the front and are made of breathable waterproof mate-

Sensible and safe turnout for a riding lesson.

rial, are the best. Nylon waterproofs that are put on over the head are often not suitable. They tend to be made of 'crackly' material and they can become hooked over the back of the saddle and restrict your movement.

■ Waterproof trousers are also unsuitable as they may be slippery and baggy.

■ Trousers should be reasonably close-fitting but not skin-tight and restrictive. Jeans are often the first choice but their hard seams can make them uncomfortable to ride in; track-suit bottoms would be a better option. Jodhpurs are best, though, as they are specifically designed to be flexible and comfortable to ride in. Shorts are totally unsuitable, even in hot weather, because bare legs can easily chafe on the saddle or stirrup leathers.

■ Your **footwear** is very important. Assuming you don't already possess purpose-made riding boots or jodhpur boots, make sure the shoes you wear are sturdy. This is essential as you will be moving around the horse and he could tread on you (which is unlikely if you are well taught). The shoes must also be strong enough not to slip through the stirrups. Ideally, wear some walking-type shoes with laces rather than buckles, which could catch on the stirrup. The shoe should have a small heel and minimal tread on the sole. Heavy-ridged soles are not suitable. Likewise, trainers are totally unsuitable and should not be worn. Short, ankle-length boots are good for riding in, and there are some useful 'paddock boots' on the market which either lace up or have elasticated sides.

■ It is essential that any clothing you wear is not likely to come loose while you are riding and then flap around dangerously. A scarf, if worn, must be tied or tucked well into your sweater or coat. Coats should always be done up, not open and flapping. A loose, flapping coat or other garment could frighten a horse and cause an upset.

■ Jewellery, other than a watch and a close-fitting smooth ring, is not appropriate for riding. Earrings should be tiny, unobtrusive studs. Dangling earrings or hoops can be dangerous if they catch on anything. Bangles and bracelets, if worn, should be of the open-ended type that will pull off in an emergency.

■ It is advisable not to wear strong perfume or aftershave while riding as it can upset some horses.

■ **A riding hat is essential**. Much research has been done in recent years on the safety of equipment used for riding, and riding hats carry a BSI (British Standards Institution) endorsement to verify their quality to give maximum protection for the job for which they are designed. Your riding school should advise you on what they require.

It is wise to purchase your own riding hat at the earliest opportunity after you decide that riding is for you. Many establishments insist that you have your own hat at the outset; some schools will lend or hire a hat to you as long as you accept responsibility for its fit. When you purchase a hat, make sure

Trainers are totally unacceptable for riding. They are unsafe in stirrups, as they can slip through the iron. If a horse treads on you when you are wearing trainers, the result is very painful!

A well-fitted riding hat.

This hat is sitting too far back on the rider's head and would not give correct or adequate protection in the event of a fall.

that you buy it from a saddler or other shop where a qualified hat-fitter can give you advice on size and fit and sell you a hat that is fit for the purpose.

■ If you normally wear contact lenses or spectacles for everyday activities, then it is generally safe and acceptable to wear them when riding. If in doubt, ask your riding school for advice.

■ Gloves are not essential but wearing them is a good habit to develop. In winter your hands will be warmer; and later on, if you aspire to compete in dressage, they are compulsory. Your school can advise on the type you need.

Understanding the horse's tack

From your very first lesson, you need to understand something about the saddlery – known as 'tack' – that your horse will normally wear. (You should, however, always be assisted in the initial stages.)

When you know which horse you have been allocated to ride, you should find him waiting for you with his tack on.

You should be shown very early on how to lead the horse (see next chapter).

The following information should help you recognise your horse's tack and begin to understand how to use it.

The horse should be wearing:

■ A simple **snaffle bridle**.

■ A **saddle** (usually a 'general-purpose' type).

The **bridle** fits comfortably over the horse's head and the snaffle bit lies in the horse's mouth across the fleshy bulk of his tongue. From the top of his head, the parts of the snaffle bridle can be described as follows:

■ The **headpiece** – this sits over the horse's head, snugly behind his ears, the **throatlatch** does up loosely under the horse's neck to keep the bridle in place.

■ The **browband**, as the name suggests, sits on the forehead; it prevents the bridle from slipping backwards.

■ There are two **cheekpieces**, which lie against the horse's cheeks and attach the headpiece to the bit.

■ The **noseband** – this goes round the nose and jaw and may be decorative or functional, depending on the design and how it is fitted. A **cavesson** is the mildest type and the most common.

■ The **bit** lies in the mouth and is attached to the cheekpieces and the reins.

■ The **reins** – these should be around the neck when the horse is being ridden, but they are taken (forward) over the head to enable the horse to be led in hand.

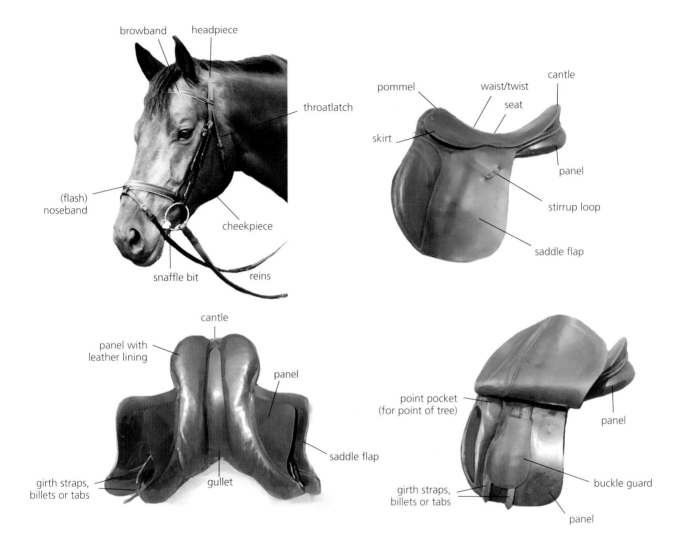

The **saddle** sits on the horse's back just behind the withers. The weight of the saddle and the rider are taken over the broad back muscles either side of the horse's spine. The saddle comprises:

- The **tree**, which is not visible but is the 'skeleton' of the saddle and the leather work is built up around it.

- The **pommel**, which is the front arch of the saddle; this is immediately in front of you when you sit in the saddle.

- The **cantle**, which is behind you at the back of the seat.

- The **seat**, which is the deep surface area on which you sit.

- The **stirrup leathers** – these hang from the stirrup bars, which are permanently and securely attached to the tree. The stirrup leathers carry the **stirrup irons**.

- The **girth** – this keeps the saddle in place on the horse's back.

THE POINTS OF THE HORSE

The different parts of the horse's body – such as the withers, hock and muzzle – are known collectively as the 'points'. A basic knowledge of these points can be useful in your lessons.

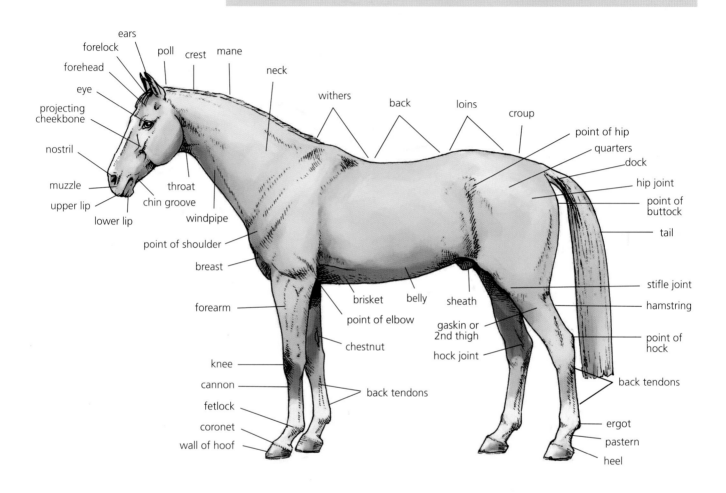

YOUR OWN FITNESS

Riding is a sport. To engage in any sport you must have some commitment to your own fitness. The horse will find it much easier to carry an active, flexible weight rather than a heavy, inactive uncoordinated one. While riding itself is a form of exercise, if you already have a basic level of fitness through, say, walking the dog, swimming or cycling, you will find it helps tremendously in your enjoyment of your new sport.

Additional items that you might encounter at this stage include:

- A **numnah** – this is a shaped pad of material (such as synthetic fleece, felt or cotton) or sheepskin, which sits under the saddle and is designed to offer the horse some cushioning for his back.

- A **neck strap** – a strap of leather which is worn round the horse's neck to provide an extra handhold for added security (especially when being lunged or when jumping).

- A **martingale** – a device to prevent the horse from raising his head too high and out of the angle of control.

- A **headcollar** – a leather or webbing device which is fastened over the horse's head. With a rope attached under the chin, it is used for leading or tying up.

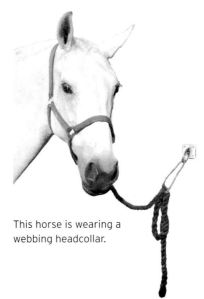

This horse is wearing a webbing headcollar.

chapter 3

Learning the basics

Leading in hand

Learning how to lead a horse in hand is one of the most important and enduring lessons you will ever learn with regard to riding horses.

Every time you ride or exercise a horse he has to be collected from wherever he is, and afterwards, taken back again. For example, he may have to be:

- brought in from the field;

- taken out to the field;

- taken from his stable to the school to mount and ride;

- taken back to his stable or field after riding;

and each time he will have to be led.

While this task is often undertaken by staff at the riding school, the sooner you can learn to do this **competently** and **confidently**, the more you will feel in control of your horse and the more positive you will feel about being around horses. Care should be taken to show you exactly how to master this apparently simple task. Then, with time and repetition, you will develop more ability and your confidence will grow.

To lead a horse with a bridle

When you first start leading in hand there should always be someone there to help you. Your instructor should take you through the procedure (see the illustrations opposite):

- Begin by taking the reins over the horse's head (unless the horse is wearing a martingale – see photo on opposite page).

- Horses are usually led from the nearside (their left), so make sure you stand on that side. In the right hand, which is close to the horse's head, hold both

Leading a bridled horse in hand, with the reins taken over his head.

This horse is wearing a running martingale, so to lead him correctly the reins are left in place around his neck.

reins firmly but not tightly together; in the left hand firmly hold the end of the reins near the buckle end.

- Stand quite close to the horse (not quite touching him) and about level with halfway down his neck. (Don't position yourself too far forward or you will discourage him from coming with you.)

- You should then walk purposefully forward and **expect** the horse to come with you. Avoid looking back appealingly at the horse hoping he will take pity on you and follow – he won't. You must adopt an air of authority and not question that the horse will come with you. By nature, horses are followers; they are not deliberately wilful. However, they sometimes choose to set their own agenda, but only if you lack authority over them. However timid you may feel, put your 'best foot forward' and stride out with purpose.

- Start and stop as you choose. It may help to say 'walk on' (with firmness and authority), and 'whoa' when you want him to stop. When you stop firmly, expect him to do so as well.

- If following behind another horse, make you sure you don't get too close. Stay out of range and be prepared to stop if the horse in front stops.

- On reaching the school where you will be riding, line up with the other horses and riders (usually on the centre line or just in off the track) and halt.

If at any stage when leading, you feel anxious or out of control, ask for assistance. A good instructor should be keeping a careful eye on his ride and be quick to observe and act if anyone needs support.

Leading in and out from the riding area should become an integral part of your riding experience. Work to perfect your handling technique (control of the rein) and enjoy the increasing authority that accompanies good leading.

In fact, leading efficiently helps to instil greater confidence in your overall dealings with the horse and he will quickly begin to respect you. If he thinks you are an 'easy touch' and that he can pull the reins away from you and grab

Leading the horse safely out of the stable with the door wide open and the horse walking straight.

SHERRY

Leading in ride order after a lesson. Note the distance between each horse and the controlled single file for safety.

a bite of grass on the way to the school, then he may 'try it on' at any given opportunity, whether he is unmounted or being ridden.

Start as you mean to go on and assert yourself as 'the boss'. The horse should then be a willing and compliant partner.

It is important, particularly when in a group, that riders always line up safely to mount and dismount. Develop the habit of lining up in a straight line with a suitable gap between each horse (horses should not be able to reach each other easily and touch noses). Your instructor should insist on this procedure, but in any case develop good habits that will hold you in good stead when the time comes eventually for you to ride independently or to line up to mount without your instructor being immediately present. By lining up safely you minimise the risk of horses:

- bumping into each other because they are too close;

- getting irritated with each other because they are too close;

- getting kicked or trodden on because they are too close.

Horses well disciplined in this procedure are less likely to be unruly or to 'barge' in their effort to return to the stables.

Mounting and dismounting

The words 'mounting' and 'dismounting' are traditional terms which are still very widely used in horse circles to describe getting on and getting off your horse.

Mounting and dismounting (which you will need to do **every** time you ever ride a horse) are two of the **most** important things to learn to do well as a rider of any level. This is because poor mounting (and to a lesser degree poor dismounting) can result in:

- discomfort to the horse which may cause further problems;
- displacement or damage to the saddle;
- damage to the horse's back;
- damage to the rider's back;
- lack of control, which may result in further problems.

Preparing to mount

Having led the horse out to the arena there are some preparatory things which need to be done before you attempt to mount. These are:

- Take the reins (which you have used to lead the horse) over the horse's head so they are in place for when you are riding. Once you have done this, keep one hand linked through the reins; never drop the reins and leave the horse standing completely free (he might decide to walk off!)
- Check the girth. Do this by feeling under it with your hand. If it is a little slack, pull the girth straps up gently but firmly until the girth is secure enough for you to mount without the saddle slipping. Your instructor should advise on the degree of tightness that you need.
- Pull down both stirrup leathers so that the irons are hanging down, ready for use when you mount.

All these tasks should be clearly explained by your instructor and help offered so that you complete them correctly. These measures help to ensure that the equipment and the horse are safe to mount.

Checking the stirrup for the approximate correct riding length.

Checking the girth before mounting to ensure that it is secure.

Tightening the girth. Note that the rider still has control of the horse because she is holding the reins.

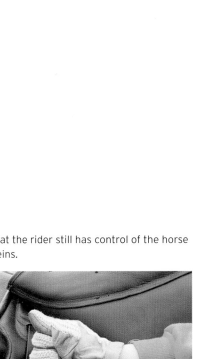

Mounting

Once the preparatory tasks are completed, you will be shown how to mount the horse. This will be done either through a demonstration by your instructor, or by your instructor taking you step by step through the procedure. From here on, you must practise your mounting procedure so that you do it a little better every time and with more confidence.

The following points and accompanying illustrations should help you to complete the mounting procedure competently.

■ Mounting is generally carried out from the nearside of the horse (his left).

■ Take up the reins, place them in the left hand and rest the hand on the horse's neck. Gather a piece of mane as well so that your left hand is secure.

■ Stand with your back to the horse's head and take the stirrup on the nearside into your right hand.

Mounting procedure.
1. Take the stirrup in the right hand and stand with your back to the horse's head, keep the reins in the left hand and grab a chunk of mane if necessary.
2. Place the left foot in the stirrup - without poking the horse in the ribs.
3. Spring up with energy, at the same time taking hold of the panel of the saddle on the offside.
4. Swing your right leg clearly over the horse's hindquarters, without touching him, and allow your weight to settle gently into the saddle; place your foot in the offside stirrup.

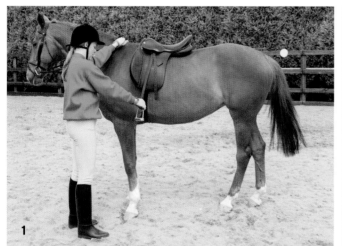

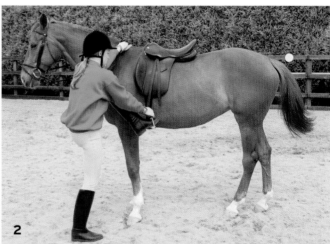

- Put your left toe into the stirrup and, without pushing your toe into the horse's side, push your toe downwards a little.

- Spring two or three times off your right foot – this should give you some 'lift' to propel you up into the air.

- Simultaneously with the impetus of the spring and the lift into the air, swing your right leg up and over the horse's rump to put yourself astride the horse.

- Keep control of your weight and lower your seat gently into the saddle, then feel for the offside stirrup.

- Pick up the reins in both hands.

Dismounting

The dismounting procedure is itemised below, point by point, to give you a mental check-list which you can run through every time you practise. Usually the horse is at a standstill (and this is essential for a beginner rider).

- Take both reins into the left hand, leaving the right hand free. Place the right hand to the right of the pommel (front of the saddle).

- Take both feet out of your stirrups.

- Swing your upper body forward and, at the same time, swing your right leg

Dismounting.
1. Take both reins into the left hand, leaving the right hand free. Place the right hand to the right of the pommel.
2. Take your feet out of the stirrups. Swing your upper body forward and, at the same time, swing your right leg cleanly over the horse's hindquarters (without kicking him on the bottom).
3 Land on the nearside of the horse with bent knees to absorb the shock of jumping down. Keep hold of the reins.

smoothly over the horse's hindquarters (high enough to be clear with no risk of kicking him on the bottom). These two actions should be fluent and coordinated.

- Land on the nearside of the horse with bent knees to absorb the shock of jumping down. Keep hold of the reins.

- 'Run up' both stirrups so that they are safe for leading the horse back to the stable (you will be shown how to do this).

- Loosen the girth to improve the horse's comfort and aid relaxation after his work.

- Take the reins over the horse's head, so that you can use them to lead him back to the stables.

During the first few lessons help should be on hand to ensure that you become competent and confident in tasks linked to safe mounting and dismounting. If working in a group you should always line up in a straight line where the horses will be safe and not able to disturb each other while the riders take time practising their mounting and dismounting.

Alternative ways to mount

There are alternative ways to mount the horse and these can be listed as:

- Mounting from a mounting block (or similar). This makes mounting easier if you are quite small and the horse is big, or if you lack agility.

- Mounting by receiving a 'leg-up' (see photos below). In this case someone, usually your instructor, assists you to spring onto the horse by physically giving you a 'lift'. You are given support under your left leg and make your spring a combined effort.

Giving and receiving a 'leg-up'. The rider must spring up with agility from the light assistance of the person giving the leg-up.

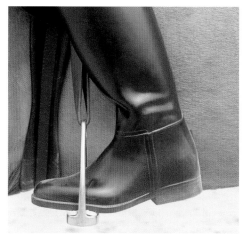
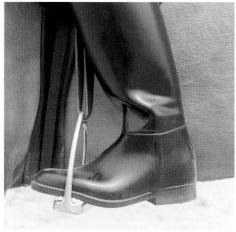

Stirrup leather twisted, with edge of leather against the leg.

Stirrup leather lying flat against the leg.

Putting your feet in the stirrups

Once on board, you need to be sure that your stirrups are set at a comfortable length. At first these should be adjusted for you. In due course, you will learn to gauge and adjust your own stirrups when you mount.

Make sure that your seat is as much in the centre of the saddle as possible, stretch both legs down the horse's side and then carry your toe up, with the heel staying a little deeper than the toe. Avoid thinking of pushing your heel down as this tends to make your ankle stiff and tight.

When your legs hang down the side of the horse in a relaxed way, the stirrup will hang close to your leg and the bottom of the stirrup iron should be in the vicinity of your ankle joint. If you then bring your leg up a little and slide your toe into the stirrup iron, the stirrups (which must be the same length on both sides) should be approximately the correct length for you to ride comfortably.

The stirrup leather should lie flat against your leg. This will happen if you learn to slip your toe into the stirrup iron by catching the stirrup between your foot and the horse's side. Don't try to find the iron by hooking your foot outwards, as this encourages a twist in the leather, which is very uncomfortable when riding. Also avoid looking down and holding the stirrup leather with one hand (even in the early stages) because this too can cause the leather to twist. Learn instead to feel for your stirrups.

Rider assessing stirrup length. If the irons rest against the ankle bones then the length is approximately correct.

Tightening the girth and adjusting stirrup length

Before you can even think of moving off, you will need to check the girth. It is essential to do this after mounting, and then again after a few minutes. In the early stages your instructor will certainly help you with this, but it is perfectly possible to do it yourself, from the saddle. Place both reins into your right hand, swing your left leg forward (see photo overleaf) and lean down to grasp

Adjusting the stirrup while mounted, keeping the foot in the stirrup for ease of movement and safety.

The instructor is looking to see if the rider's stirrups are level. This is easy to check from the ground.

Tightening the girth while mounted. Note the control through the reins while the left hand is adjusting the girth.

the girth strap with your left hand. Pull up each girth strap, one at a time, and rebuckle to the desired tension.

If you find you need to alter your stirrup length, you can also do this yourself while in the saddle. Your instructor will show you how it should be done, and then you'll have to practise the technique. Keep your feet in the stirrups whenever you do this. With the reins in one hand, use your free hand to pull the stirrup leather buckle out from under your leg. Change the length as required, rebuckle the leather, and pull on the inner leather strap to bring the buckle back up to the top (otherwise it will feel uncomfortable under your leg).

The basic riding position

You are 'sitting' on the horse, astride, with one foot in each stirrup. Now you must take some time to think about **how** you are sitting.

- Are you sitting in the way you would sit in an armchair at home?

- Are you sitting the way you would on a bicycle (but not the type with dropped handlebars)?

- Are you sitting straight-backed and to attention?

- Are you sitting in a slumped way, leaning back and/or sideways?

If these questions have made you think that there is more than one way to 'sit' then I have achieved my aim.

A good basic riding position. The vertical line shows the balance of the rider from ear, through shoulder, hip and to the heel.

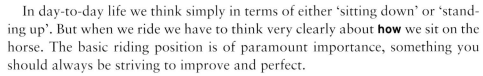

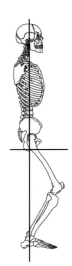

Correct basic position

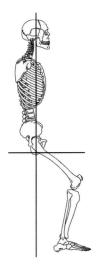

Collapsed, armchair seat

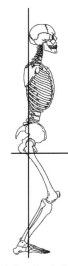

Hollow back, fork seat

In day-to-day life we think simply in terms of either 'sitting down' or 'standing up'. But when we ride we have to think very clearly about **how** we sit on the horse. The basic riding position is of paramount importance, something you should always be striving to improve and perfect.

In thinking about **how** we sit on the horse, one factor we always need to bear in mind is that the horse is constantly 'moving' even if he is standing still – he is alive, thinking, breathing and 'animate'.

The reasons for aiming to adopt a good basic riding position are:

■ To enable the horse to carry the rider with minimum effort.

■ To enable the rider to maintain optimum effect and balance.

■ To enable the rider to communicate harmoniously with the horse through a clear system of aids (signals or messages).

In fact, a good position is the basis for developing your ability as a rider.

Here are some of the qualities that make up a good position:

■ The rider should be **sitting squarely** in the lowest part of the saddle, his point of balance very close to that of the horse (i.e. behind the withers).

■ The upper body should be **tall**; the head not dropped forward – rather a feeling of the neck drawn back into the rider's collar; with relaxation of the shoulders and therefore the upper arm and forearm.

■ The hands should be **relaxed**, and closed around the reins, with the **thumbs uppermost** and the wrists straight, not curled inwards.

■ The rider's weight should be taken **equally** on both seat bones, the legs hang-

Rider sitting straight and level in the saddle

Rider leaning to the right. This collapses the right hip and pushes the seat bones to the left of the saddle.

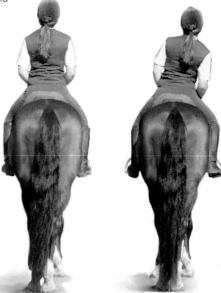

ing evenly down the horse's side, with the ball of the foot resting on the stirrup, and the heel a little deeper than the toe.

■ If the position is viewed from the side, there should be **two imaginary straight lines** (during your lessons you will find these are often referred to by riding instructors) as follows:

■ a **vertical line** which runs from the rider's ear, through the shoulder, through the hip, and down to the heel;

and

■ a **straight line** which runs from the elbow, through the wrist, to the horse's mouth (via the rein).

Rider leaning back, lower leg forward and position out of balance

Rider perched forward with back hollow and lower leg rather tight.

WORKING TO ACHIEVE A GOOD RIDING POSITION

A good riding position is something that every committed rider spends his entire life striving for. Just as in golf, where a good golf swing is so important, so in riding the basic position is the foundation for the development of a competent and effective rider. It is something that should be addressed (one way or another) in every riding lesson you have. Achieving a good riding position comes from:

- An understanding of how to sit on the horse and of the basic position you are trying to adopt.
- Working to maintain that position at halt and in movement.
- Constantly self-correcting any small faults that arise.
- Practising the 'feel' of sitting well and noticing how much more effective you can be when you do sit well.
- Taking every opportunity to check your position – by looking at yourself in mirrors in the school, by studying video feedback taken by your family or friends, and by being self-motivated and working hard to improve your body alignment whenever you ride.
- Regular exercises to improve suppleness and therefore coordination in your riding.
- Regular work without stirrups – this (as you will discover later) will improve your balance, your security in the saddle and your 'feel' of the horse.

It is often helpful to have the correct position demonstrated to you, along with common faults that might occur, e.g. leaning backwards, leaning forwards, etc.

Once on board, the instructor will help you to adopt a basically correct position in the saddle. Remember, though, that everyone is different, and that it takes time to develop a good position. Your aim must be to work at improving your position through practice and feedback from your instructor.

A more comprehensive description of the rider's basic position is given in *The BHS Manual of Equitation*, a book you may want to read when you are truly hooked on riding and want to progress.

Ultimately achieving a good 'seat' is being able to maintain a sound, basic riding position throughout any movement made by the horse, whether expected or not, so that your balance is never out of harmony with the horse. Now back to the early lessons!

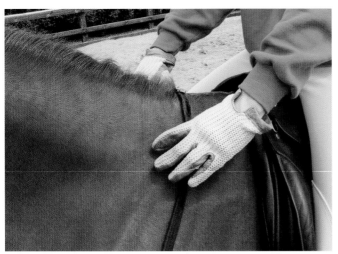

How to pick up and hold the reins correctly.

Holding the reins

Having adopted a comfortable position in the saddle you must next learn how to pick up and hold the reins.

The reins should be lying on the horse's neck (in front of the saddle). Place your hands over the reins (as if going to play a piano, **not** underneath as if picking up a book) and take one rein in each hand. Slip your little finger to the outside of the rein, and turn your hand upwards and outwards so that the

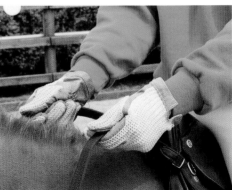

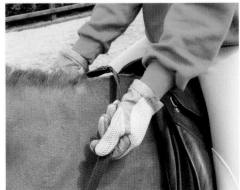

How **not** to hold the reins. **ABOVE** Stiff, set hands. **RIGHT (BOTH PHOTOS)** Reins picked up incorrectly, from underneath.

thumb comes to the top and the back of your hand is in line with the back of your arm. Imagine you have a baby bird in each hand: you want to hold it firmly enough not to allow it to fly away, but not so tightly that you squash it. Your thumbs should always be uppermost on top of the rein. Your thumb can then act as a 'stop' on the rein: if your thumb is light you can let the rein slip through the hand and make it longer; if your thumb is closed and firm against the rein, you can prevent the rein from being 'taken' by the horse and you can keep the rein shorter when you need to.

Your hands will generally be held above the horse's withers (just in front of the saddle) about two or three inches apart from each other but otherwise at the same height and level, and as a pair.

You will find that the length of your reins is constantly changing and that shortening and lengthening the reins is something that you will have to learn to do constantly while you are riding.

Lengthening the reins is easy and is done as described above.

To shorten the reins you need to take the reins into one hand and then move the free hand down its respective rein to shorten it, then take the reins in the other hand (keeping the shorter rein length) and shorten the second rein in the same way. This takes practice, and it may help you to find a piece of washing line (a long dog's lead will do) and sit at home practising the technique so that the next time you ride you are more proficient at this task.

How to shorten the reins (see text above).

Introducing the system of aids

In the early stages, you should be given minimal information to assimilate (so as not to overload you) but you will be taught about the system of aids. These are the messages or signals which we use to communicate with the horse while we are riding.

When riding we give aids (send signals to the horse) by contact, pressure, or influence of:

- the seat;

- the legs;

- the hands;

- the voice.

These are known as the natural aids.

In addition to natural aids are artificial aids, which are applied through items of equipment:

- whips;

- spurs;

- martingales (these are pieces of horse tack which may be used to influence the horse's head carriage).

You will learn much more about the aids and how to apply them as you work through this book.

chapter 4

Early lessons

However keen you are to learn to ride, once you are sitting on top of a living creature (about five or six feet off the ground) with very little (if any) idea of how to control him, you may have some doubts about your initial enthusiasm! Don't be daunted – you should have a leader and/or instructor very close at hand to tell you very clearly what you should be doing. The horse chosen for your early lessons should be well acquainted with teaching beginner riders. He should be calm and equable and quite used to waiting patiently for instructions from his inexperienced pilot.

Starting and stopping

Moving off

Having picked up the reins, the way to ask the horse to move forward is to give the following aid: use both legs to apply pressure (squeeze) against the horse's side. The beginner rider will probably not have either the coordination or the balance to apply a smooth, gentle squeeze, which is the ultimate aim. Horses, however, do respond differently to varying pressure from this aid, and in the first instance you may need to give a small 'kick' or nudge with the lower part of your leg and heel against the horse's side. As you do this, try not to allow your whole body to move as well, and keep your hands quiet and still. The horse should move forward when:

- You sit still, maintaining your good position, then give a small kick or inward nudge (or ideally a squeeze) with both legs.

Don't get busy with your hands, just allow the horse to respond and walk forward. He must not feel a restricting rein at this time; the reins must allow him to go forward.

In the initial few moments of moving forward for the first time, allow yourself to experience the feel of the horse under you. Riding is all about 'feel', so continually be aware of what you can feel.

Stopping (halting)

So now you are moving forward you will want to be able to **stop!** (In the horse world we call this 'halting'.) The following procedure will almost certainly ensure that you have the ability to stop when you want to.

▪ Shorten both reins a little. Invariably the reins will slip and become a little long, so as a preparation to stop it is wise to shorten the reins so that the aid when given is clear and you can keep your position.

▪ Correct and maintain your basic position. Sit tall in the saddle.

▪ Feel the contact of both your legs around the horse's side and give a consistent but gentle restricting squeeze on both reins to prevent the horse from continuing to go forward.

▪ It is vital that the reins are short enough so that the horse feels a 'closing hand' not a pulling back hand.

▪ As soon as the horse responds (in this case from walk to halt) then the restrictive pressure through the rein should be released so that the horse is rewarded for the correct response and the aid is no longer applied.

The aids for stopping and starting are 'tools' that you will use within your

Rider showing a pleasing basic position at the halt; the horse is standing in a balanced way over all his four feet.

riding for the rest of the time you choose to enjoy this sport. Your aim should therefore be to practise and refine your ability to apply these aids effectively with every horse you ride. You will find that horses respond differently to these aids. Some are very responsive, others are lazier, and you will learn to be firmer with a lazy horse and more passive with a 'sharper' one. This is one of the challenges and continual stimulations of riding. No two horses are the same, and you will learn something different from every horse you ride. Feel confident about this as an aspect of the sport you have chosen.

ABOVE LEFT Rider with the reins too short, which straightens and tightens her arms and pulls her shoulders into a rather hunched position.
ABOVE Rider with reins too long, hands pulling back and the lower leg then slipping forward out of balance.

Turning right and left

You are now ready to learn the basics of turning. Adding this to your repertoire means that, to all intents and purposes, you have the rudiments required for developing your ability as a rider: you can get on and off the horse, you can stop and start and you can turn left and right. The rest is just building on those skills to whatever level you aspire – and, of course, lots of practice.

As you learn how to ride a turn you will become more aware of the need to coordinate your aids. Because, as a novice rider, your balance and coordination will not be easily under your control, much of your early lessons will be aimed at improving the security of your position and therefore your ability to give your aids clearly to the horse.

Let's consider how you should go about asking the horse to turn:

- Whenever you require the horse to change direction try to get into the habit of using your legs before giving any rein aids which might be required.

- Before you give any new 'message' to the horse, it is always wise to check the length of your reins and shorten them if necessary.

- An effective squeeze with both legs, evenly on the horse's side (or, as previ-

Good hand position with wrists relaxed, thumbs uppermost and fingers relaxed but around the rein. The rein aids are applied with a take-and-give (squeeze-and-give) action. The hand must never pull backwards or hold.

ously discussed, until the 'squeeze' is perfected, a short, sharp 'kick' against the horse's side to make him think forward), precedes a left or right rein aid.

■ Asking the horse to turn involves the rider 'squeezing' the appropriate rein (left rein for a left turn, right rein for a right turn) in a motion that I can only describe as being like pulling against a stretchy piece of strong elastic. The rider should 'feel' a positive elastic contact at the end of the rein and the horse's head should follow the direction asked by the rein. The rider should see the horse's inside eyelid (right or left according to the direction asked) and should 'feel' a similar (elastic) connection in the outside rein (opposite to the direction of the bend).

■ In turning left (for example) the rider uses both legs to maintain the forward energy in the pace, applies the left rein to ask the horse to turn and at the same time allows with the outside (right) rein while not abandoning its contact completely, but enough to enable the horse to bend through the turn.

■ As the turn is completed the left rein (known as the 'inside rein' because it is on the inside of the turn) is released a little (i.e. it no longer asks for the increased direction) and the supporting right rein (known as the 'outside rein') comes more into play to help straighten the horse after the turn. The rider will need to use both legs again as necessary, to maintain the forward-ness of the turn.

■ If the inside rein (in this case, the left) is not released a little after the turn, the

PRACTICE, PRACTICE, PRACTICE . . .

In your first few lessons much emphasis should be put on your practice of:

■   Shortening and lengthening the reins.

■   Stopping and starting.

■   Turning left and right.

The horse 'straight'.

The horse with a consistent bend through his whole body.

In both cases the inside hind leg would follow the inside foreleg and the outside hind leg would follow the outside foreleg.

horse will continue to turn through more of an arc than is required.

Turns are ridden in walk at first, then as your competence develops they can be ridden in any gait.

In the early lessons you may find that you have to think through each phase of the movement. Do not be dismayed – these movements will become easier with practice.

A rider showing a fair position in walk; the horse has three legs in contact with the ground and only the right foreleg is clearly in the air.

Halt and walk

Horses used for teaching beginner riders should feel very comfortable about standing still, and waiting in halt. They must, however, be willing enough to move forward from halt easily and generously when asked. The horse must stand still (halt) patiently for as long as it takes for you to mount and have your stirrups adjusted; he must then move forward and halt again as often as you want him to. He should stand still for as long as you require him to. Walk will be the gait that you spend most, if not all of your first lesson, using; it should also be a gait that you come back to frequently to re-establish your position and balance. Here we will take a moment to consider the halt and the walk to give you a greater understanding of what the horse is doing.

Halt

When the horse distributes his weight evenly over his four legs he is 'in balance'. At a standstill this is fairly easy for him, but when we put a rider on top, he then has to balance his own weight and that of his rider. One of the reasons we try so hard to maintain 'a good basic position' on the horse is because he will then find it easier to balance himself. As you ride:

■ Learn to 'feel' how the horse halts and whether there is a 'feeling' of him being in balance over his four legs.

■ Learn to encourage the horse to find his own balance when he halts. Sometimes when he stops you will feel him move a leg or 'shuffle' to adjust his balance – don't worry about this movement; allow it to happen. (See the later exercise on feeling the hind legs.)

■ Your instructor should encourage you from your earliest lesson to identify as much as possible what your horse is doing underneath you. This will help you to feel familiar with the horse and how he moves.

Walk

The horse has four gaits (also called paces). The walk is the slowest of these; the others are trot, canter and gallop. Walk, trot and canter are the gaits with which you will become most familiar in your early riding lessons.

The walk is a lovely gait and often overlooked in favour of the 'faster, more fun' gaits. It is a gait that you should feel entirely comfortable in and one that you can return to to take a breather from more energetic parts of your lesson. In walk you:

■ Have time to think about what you have done.

■ Can check on your own position and make minor corrections to it.

■ Can think about preparing for your next activity, e.g. about the aids you may need to give for your next change of pace or to ride your next exercise.

Later on, walk will be a gait that you can enjoy when hacking out or on a holiday trek, as it gives you time to appreciate the countryside as you go. (See Chapter 9.)

The horse's walk is easy to sit on because:

- It is a relatively slow gait.

- At any one time the horse has three feet on the ground supporting his weight, and there is no moment when all his feet are off the ground at the same time (as in trot and canter), so the pace is very smooth.

In walk the horse's legs move in the following sequence:

- **1**. right hind;

- **2**. right fore;

- **3**. left hind;

- **4**. left fore;

- **5**. sequence repeats.

ABOVE LEFT Free walk on a long rein. The rein is long but contact is still maintained with the horse's mouth.
ABOVE Walk on a loose rein. The rider is holding just the buckle end of the reins. The only connection with the horse's mouth is the weight of the rein, otherwise the contact is completely loose.

TRY THIS EXERCISE

An interesting exercise which you can use to develop your 'feel' of the horse walking under you, is to identify which leg is moving at any one time and then try to notice those movements in your own seat or body which repeat with the movement of the leg underneath you.

Starting to trot

No doubt you have seen horses trotting, with or without a rider. If you watch closely you will see that the trot is a two-time gait, in which the horse's legs move in diagonal pairs. The legs move in the following sequence:

1. Left foreleg with the right hind leg (named the **left diagonal**).

2. Moment of suspension (when all four legs are in the air with no contact with the ground).

3. Right foreleg with the right hind leg (named the **right diagonal**).

Because of the moment of suspension and the activity of the horse lifting from one pair of legs to the other, trot has a definite 'spring' or bounce to it, and obviously it is faster than the walk.

If you have never trotted before then having your first experience of trot should be fun, exciting and challenging. It is an easy and gentle progression from halt and walk.

Whether your first trot experience will come in your first lesson will be dependent on many circumstances and is different for every new rider. Some of the things which should be considered are:

■ Your confidence. How keen are you to trot? If in doubt, there is **no** hurry.

■ How easily have you grasped the leading in hand, mounting, learning the basics of how to sit, stopping and starting, and turning left and right? Taking that list into account then it would not be unusual not to trot for several lessons, but if you are keen to progress and your instructor thinks you are ready, then 'go for it'.

A relaxed partnership riding outside. Rider showing a fair basic position on a well-balanced horse in trot.

- The likelihood is that if you are in a group of beginner riders, several of the group will want to trot and the lesson will therefore progress towards that goal.

Your instructor should ask you the following questions:

- Have you trotted before?

- Have you seen trot?

- Do you know the difference between sitting and rising trot?

Let us assume that the answers to those questions are 'no', 'yes' and 'yes' respectively.

By explaining the nature of the trot gait (as described above) your instructor should make you aware of why the trot is bouncy and why trot can be ridden sitting or rising.

At first you should just learn to experience the 'feel' of the trot. Without making any more effort than to relax in the centre of the saddle and trying to maintain your basic position, you prepare to move the horse into trot. (Remember: your leader or lunger will have ultimate control of the horse, but it is preferable that you practise giving the appropriate aids yourself, right from the start.)

The aids from walk to trot are:

- Make sure that the walk is active.

- Shorten your reins, and make a mental note to correct your basic position.

- Give a positive squeeze with both legs against the horse's side, or, if necessary, a short, sharp kick with both legs, to tell the horse to go forward from walk into trot.

- Let the reins allow (without them going slack) the horse to go forward into the trot.

Sitting trot

In sitting trot the rider absorbs the bouncy movement of the trot through suppleness and relaxation while maintaining a good basic position.

Ideally the horse chosen for the beginner or novice rider will not have an extravagant trot, which would be more difficult to learn to sit on.

When first trying sitting trot there may be a tendency for beginners to stiffen and then the following faults are likely to creep in:

- The lower leg grips the horse and the toe turns out as the tight leg pushes the rider up off the saddle.

- The hands become unsteady and jerky, no longer staying still above the horse's withers.

- As balance is lost in the saddle so is basic security, and the rider tips forwards or backwards and loses position.

Trot should be practised in small bouts so that these faults can be worked on in the intervening periods of walk. Each time, the rider should have the opportunity to practise the whole sequence:

- Correct the position and relax as the preparation to trot is made (shorten reins).

- Give the aids to trot.

- Practise trot.

- Return to walk.

- Reassess position and repeat the whole procedure.

Much of the control for this sequence will be taken by either the leader or the instructor lungeing the horse. Beginner riders should have to concentrate only minimally on the control of the horse and a great deal on their own position and use of the aids.

If your hands are unsteady, you should be encouraged to rest them (while still holding the reins correctly) on the pommel of the saddle so that in trot they do not interfere with the horse. Gradually from this more secure position you can practise taking one hand at a time off the saddle and into the correct rein

---

TRANSITIONS

Changes of gait, as discussed throughout this book, are called **transitions**. Transitions are a basic tool for riding horses whether to school and train them to more advanced work or purely to ride them for leisure and enjoyment. Transitions are either upward or downward. **Upward transitions** take you from a slower to a faster gait, e.g. walk to trot, trot to canter. **Downward transitions** take you from a faster to a slower gait, e.g. trot to walk or walk to halt. All these transitions are known as **progressive transitions**, they pass from the adjacent gait to the next, upwards or downwards - walk, trot, canter. **Acute**, or **direct transitions** make changes of gait which miss out the adjacent gait and sometimes more, e.g. halt to trot, walk to canter, canter to halt.

In your early lessons you are likely only to be concerned with progressive transitions. When you ride your first dressage test (which may be at the riding school) you may have to ride from trot to halt or from walk to canter.

position. Then, gradually, as you develop enough balance, you will be able to take both hands off the saddle and keep your hands still. How quickly you will be able to trot without holding the saddle depends on your coordination, balance and confidence, and the time taken is not a measure of your future competence as a rider.

You should be confident and competent about moving from walk to trot (sitting) and back again from trot to walk, and from halt to walk, walk to trot and back down again before needing to worry about 'rising' trot.

Rising trot

Beginners often find learning to 'rise to the trot' to be the first major hurdle to overcome in their early riding career. Some might even ask – what is the purpose of learning to rise if one can perfect the art of sitting in a relaxed and secure position on the horse's back? The answer to that question may be:

- When working in trot for longer periods and when using trot as a gait for pleasure riding when out and about, the novice rider will soon become tired in sitting trot (beginner riders seldom find sitting trot either very easy or very comfortable for more than a few strides). As they tire they become 'heavier' on the horse's back. Once mastered, rising trot offers a very easy way to ride the trot for short or long periods of time, with little effort to the rider and with less stress on the horse's back.

How to tackle the task of learning to rise to the trot:

- First watch other riders in rising trot – it looks quite easy, and it is.

- The movement of the horse promotes the action, that is why the method of riding the trot has evolved – the two-time movement (as previously

Rising trot. The diagonal pair of legs which are touching the ground as the rider sits, is the diagonal on which the rider is riding (named from the front leg). This rider is on the left diagonal.

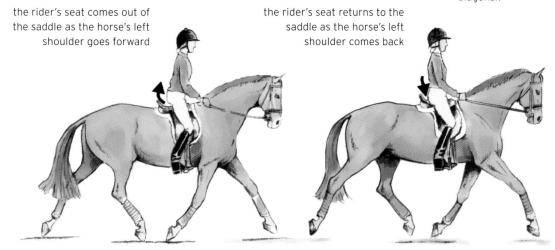

the rider's seat comes out of the saddle as the horse's left shoulder goes forward

the rider's seat returns to the saddle as the horse's left shoulder comes back

Rising trot, on the lunge. Learning to ride on the lunge enables the rider to concentrate solely on his/her riding while the instructor controls the horse.

described) helps to push the rider up.

■ Once you have mastered the rhythm of the trot, you will find it quite easy to allow the horse to push your seat briefly 'up' off the saddle and then, just as briefly, to allow your seat softly to return to touch the saddle before going 'up' again.

■ The horse's movement moves you, and once you have established the 'feel' of the movement, the horse does all the work.

Your instructor should guide you as to how best to 'learn' the feeling of the rising trot. The following method works as well as any:

■ As with your first feeling of 'sitting' trot, it may help you to feel more secure if you rest both hands on the front (pommel) of the saddle while still holding the reins correctly. Your hands should lightly hold the saddle, not 'hang on for dear life'!

■ In walk (just to give you the feel of how high your seat needs to come off the saddle) push up (using a little pressure on your stirrups and the front of the saddle to give yourself a little lift) so that your seat just clears the saddle. Then let your seat return to the saddle and then go up again.

■ Your instructor should help you to appreciate the approximate speed of the rising by saying 'up/down, up/down', or 'one/two, one/two' in the speed that will be required when in trot.

■ For a beginner rider the initial feeling of getting your seat off the saddle and moving swiftly enough to match 'trot speed' is often quite difficult.

■ Once you have the general idea of the 'feel' then it is time to try it in trot. The trot itself will actually help the 'rise'.

■ As your confidence grows, you will gradually learn to let go of the support of the saddle. First release one hand into the normal rein position above the withers and then, when you can maintain security and balance, release the other hand as well. You can always drop one hand back onto the saddle if you have a brief lapse of control or feel anxious.

Your first efforts at rising trot should be short but frequent. Each time you try it you may lose balance and control of your basic position, so it is important to keep returning to walk to correct the position and then have another go. The periods in trot must be long enough, however, actually to allow you to get the hang of the rhythm and timing. If you are being led, though, the trot time may be dictated by the fitness of your leader! On the lunge you can stay in trot a little longer as long as your position does not radically deteriorate.

Each time you practise rising trot you will develop more 'feel' for when it is good and when it feels awful. Gradually the good feeling should outweigh the bad! The time it takes to master the rhythm of rising trot varies from person to person. Some riders establish the rising rhythm in one or two lessons; some take a few weeks; one or two take longer. Take the time you need. The speed with which you master rising trot is not an indicator of your talent or otherwise as a rider.

Once you have the basic ability to proceed from walk to trot, always start the trot work in 'sitting' trot and then establish rising trot. Likewise, as you prepare to move back from trot to walk, again take sitting trot as you make the transition from trot back to walk. This will ensure that you sit in harmony with the horse through the change of gait with no loss of balance as he moves from one pace to the next.

Common faults when learning rising trot are:

- The rider finds it difficult to establish a quick enough and controlled rhythm of going up and down.

- The rider goes up too far and too slowly, and so is out of sequence with the horse when coming down.

- The rider doesn't go 'up' enough and therefore is not getting sufficient 'feel' or help from the horse's natural push in the trot.

In reality, while we talk about going 'up and down' in rising trot, the movement is actually a little up and forward at the same time. This allows a freedom and fluency of the rider's hips; also the shoulders are a shade more forward than in the upright position when sitting in the saddle.

'Feel'

So far we have covered your first experiences of learning to ride. We have talked about getting on and off, starting and stopping, turning, and moving from one gait to another. There have been two repetitive themes. One is the **movement** of the horse, and therefore the need for the rider to be able to adopt a position that allows for and develops an ability to follow that movement in every situation; and the other is **feel**, which is **crucial** to riding well. Riding is all about 'feel': learning to 'feel' what the horse is doing, and, in due course, what he is 'telling you' by through how he 'feels'. I make no apology for emphasising the importance of 'feel', and the book will continue to reflect this strongly.

Using a whip

Carrying a whip while riding a horse is very commonplace. In the early stages you might have the idea that using a whip is cruel, but this is far from the case if you understand when and how to use it correctly. The horse has a thick hide, and the whip should only ever be used to reinforce the aid given by your leg if the horse is being lazy or reluctant to listen to your leg.

In the early stages of riding it is likely that you will be shown how to carry and use a 'short' whip. This is usually up to 30 ins (75 cm) in length and a fairly stocky shape, with a flat, short leather thong on the end. The whip is normally carried in your inside hand (inside to the bend of the horse – and this would usually be the inside to the direction of going in the school in your early riding work). The whip is held in one hand along with the rein. The whip should lie

How to change a schooling whip.
1. Take both reins into the hand holding the whip.
2. Tilt the whip upwards and put your spare hand over onto the shank of the whip with the thumb nearest the hand holding the whip.
3. Allow the 'new' hand to take the whip and bring it cleanly over the top of the withers.
4. Retake the reins in both hands with the whip in the 'new' hand.

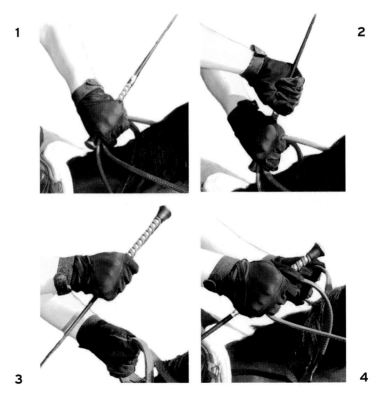

How to change a short whip. Always take the reins into one hand, leaving the hand receiving the whip free to slide the whip through over the withers onto the other side of the neck. Retake both reins.

comfortably across, and supported by, your thigh. When the whip is to be used, the reins should be taken into one hand to leave the whip hand free. The whip is then employed sharply, and once initially, along the flank of the horse, immediately behind your leg. The horse must be allowed to respond and go forward; he must not come against a restraining hand, which would contradict the message the whip has given him. If he responds forward then a rewarding pat should be given and you can resume the normal riding position with your hands.

As your competence develops then you may also be introduced to a long, or 'schooling', whip. This whip is much thinner and longer than the short whip, and has a little flicking 'tail' on the end. This whip can vary in length greatly – some are very long indeed. When you first start to use a schooling whip choose one that is not too long until you have become familiar with managing it.

The schooling whip is designed to be used without taking your hand off the rein. It can come into action on the flank just behind your leg, but it is activated by a flick of the wrist, without removing your hand from the rein. It is important that the wrist action does not interfere with the horse's mouth; and the hand must not have a backward movement in using the whip. As with the short whip, the horse must be allowed to respond forward without restriction in the mouth.

Simple suppling exercises

Exercises performed at halt and on the move are of great benefit to help the rider's position, balance, 'feel', coordination and effectiveness. They also develop confidence, enabling the rider to feel increasingly 'at home' on the horse. Different instructors use different exercises, but here are some useful ones which might be suitable for beginner and novice riders.

Exercises at halt

The following mounted exercises can be done at halt while the horse is being held, so you won't have to worry about anything other than your own movements.

Swinging the lower leg, from the knee back.

1. Slip your feet out of the stirrups, stretch your legs down long and then, without looking down, slip your toes back into the stirrups again. The stirrup leather hangs naturally, slightly at an angle from the stirrup bar, and if you 'feel' for the stirrup and catch the iron between the foot and the horse then the stirrup leather will hang correctly. If you try to hold the leather and pull the iron up to meet your foot, the chances are that you will position the stirrup leather incorrectly. A twist in the leather makes for discomfort along your leg, especially if you are not wearing long boots.

2. Put the reins down on the horse's neck and then pick them up correctly. Also practise shortening and lengthening the reins.

3. With your feet out of the stirrups, stretch one arm above your head and lean down to touch your toe, first left hand to left toe, then left hand to right toe, and similarly with the other hand. This exercise stretches your waist, makes your upper body more flexible and teaches you to keep your legs long while bending your upper body. Particularly, your outside leg must not slide back, out of position, as you bend forwards.

4. With your feet out of the stirrups, swing the lower leg (from the knee) backwards and forwards, without kicking the horse's side. This improves flexibility of the lower leg and helps prevent 'gripping' with the knees. Legs can be swung alternately or both together. (This can also be done at walk.)

5. Lean back until the back of your head touches the horse's back (this is fun for children particularly; adults can find it more daunting and difficult), then sit up, without your legs pulling up out of position. This exercise stretches and works your stomach muscles.

6. 'Around the world' is another exercise which children (particularly) enjoy. From the normal position facing forwards, you move round (by scissoring the legs from the hips) to sit sideways on the horse, then backwards, then

Arm stretches to the side improve a small child's balance and coordination. The pony is held, and the instructor is close to the child to maintain concentration.

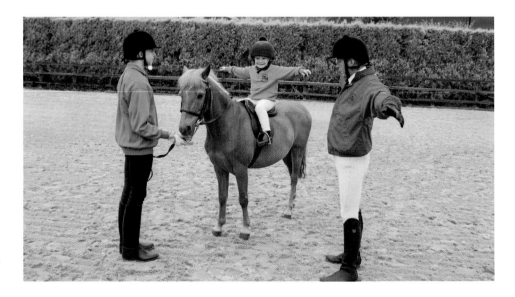

sideways on the other side of the horse, before returning to the front again. It is an exercise that requires balance, flexibility and coordination. If you can do it with your hands on your hips, then good for you!

7. Hold your arms out to the sides, parallel to the ground with shoulders back and palms facing down. Turn the upper body from side to side quite slowly until your arms are as much as possible in line with the horse's spine (one hand pointing towards the tail, the other towards the ears). This exercise supples the upper body and waist. (This can be done on the move, either on a lead rein or lunge rein.)

Exercises on the move

Exercises on the move, in walk, trot and, as you become more experienced, sometimes at canter, are fun to do and test your timing, coordination and suppleness. Your instructor should take full responsibility for choosing what exercises you can do on the move and for ultimate control of the horse, be it on the lunge rein or through a leader.

1. Take the reins in one hand and circle the other arm slowly backwards. This stretches the arm, upper body and waist and improves flexibility and coordination. Repeat with the other arm. The backward circling encourages the shoulders to be drawn back and together.

2. Shoulder-shrugging. Draw your shoulders up towards your ears, then rotate them backwards in a circling motion. This promotes relaxation in the shoulders and neck and therefore can improve hand position and rein contact.

3. Without stirrups (stirrups crossed on the horse's neck – see working without stirrups, page 71), bring both legs up in front of you with your thighs parallel to the ground. With an active thrust, push both legs down the horse's side back into position. This exercise helps to encourage a long leg and a deeper seat in the saddle.

4. Without stirrups, circle the ankles, first outwards and then with toes turning inwards. This promotes flexibility in the ankles and lower leg.

Assessing your own progress

Obviously the more often you ride, the more quickly you will progress. If you ride only once a week for 30 or 45 minutes do not worry if your progress is slow – be reassured that repetition is the key to competence and be patient in your lessons and attentive to the quality of what you do. 'Practice makes perfect' is a very true saying.

How long will you stay on the lead rein or lunge?

The answer to this question is – **as long as you need to**.

The important criteria are:

- You can lead your horse in and out from the stable to the riding area with confidence and the minimum of supervision and assistance. (There should **always** be someone competent to assist you in case you have trouble.)

- You can prepare to mount – i.e. check the girth, run down the stirrups, put the reins over the horse's head.

- You can mount with the minimum of help and make some effort to adjust your own stirrups. (Again, someone should be available to make a final adjustment to your stirrups and secure the girth if you need help before your lesson commences.)

- You can handle the reins correctly: holding them, shortening and lengthening them when necessary as you ride from halt to walk and up to trot and back down to halt.

- You can move from walk to sitting trot, into rising trot and back through sitting trot to walk, with both hands off the saddle and the hands maintaining a steady position without interfering with the horse through the transitions.

- You feel confident to work a little without your stirrups while performing some exercises at the halt and (gently) on the move.

- You can halt and dismount from your horse, then control the horse while you loosen the girth and run up your stirrups before leading him in hand back to the stables.

This level of competence might be achieved in, say, ten lessons (of half-hour duration) or it may take twenty lessons or more. The number of lessons is not indicative of your potential as a rider. No two riders are the same. Enjoy your riding and always feel satisfied with your progress – as long as you have tried your best to improve within each session and utilised the instruction that is offered to you. Never allow anyone to pressurise you into doing something you do not feel ready for or confident about 'just because everyone else in your class is doing it'.

First time off the lead rein or lunge

This should be an exciting milestone. By the time it arrives, the progression should be very easy, made possible by your developing confidence and ability. Towards the end of one of your lunge or lead-rein lessons your instructor should suggest that you have five or ten minutes 'on your own'. The horse is well used to 'looking after' his beginner pilot, so worry not. You will simply be doing everything that you have done over the past few weeks – the only difference will be that you are detached from the 'umbilical cord' that has been your life-line. On all previous occasions, your instructor (lungeing) or your leader was ultimately in charge. Now you are on your own!

Remember when you first had to drive a car without someone with you, or swim in water out of your depth having just learned to swim? Confidence is the most important thing – just tell yourself that you 'can do it' for, after all, you 'have been doing it'. You just need to be positive enough to convince the horse that you know what you are doing.

Things to do in between lessons

You may be able to ride only once a week, so what else can you do to progress your knowledge and ability without having to climb aboard your four-legged equine friend?

Fitness/exercise

While riding does not rank amongst the real energy-demanding sports, nevertheless the better your level of all-round fitness, the better your overall sense of well-being **and** your ability to obtain maximum benefit from your riding lessons. This applies to mental as well as physical fitness. Learning anything new makes heavier demands on your brain-power, so mental as well as physical agility is an advantage.

These activities can help your riding fitness:

- **Walking**. Walk to the shops. Walk to work or school (if realistic). Walk the dog.

- **Swimming**. If you enjoy swimming then the flexibility and good breathing technique that are demanded by this activity will greatly assist your riding.

- **Cycling**. Similarly, the same applies to cycling.

- **Working out at the gym**. This can help your flexibility, strength and cardio-vascular (heart and lung) fitness.

The following well-known and respected systems may also assist your riding:

- Yoga.

- Alexander Technique.

- Pilates.

If time does not allow any of the above, then think about following a basic

A series of stretching exercises, as shown here, carried out before mounting your horse, will help your suppleness and flexibility when you ride.

exercise regime at home, either when you get up in the morning or at some regular time daily. Again, this will maintain a degree of flexibility which should help your well-being and therefore your riding.

Coordination

Coordination is an essential commodity for riding. Control of the horse, as we discussed, is based on the rider's ability to communicate his messages or aids through the use of the seat, legs, hands and sometimes the voice. The more clearly you can coordinate the various aids, the more likely you are to achieve a good response from the horse. You should know whether you are naturally a well-coordinated person or not, and if you do not know then try the following exercises and they will quickly show you!

■ Try patting the top of your head with one hand and at the same time rubbing your tummy with your other hand in a circular movement. If you find this easy, then well done. If you find that as you pat your head the other hand which should be rubbing, insists on also patting, then your hands are not very well coordinated. It is fairly easy to practise this kind of exercise (without a horse in sight) to develop the ability for one hand (or leg) to do one thing while the other limb does something else.

■ Similarly, stand with both arms straight out in front of you parallel to the

Can you circle your hand, rubbing your tummy, and, at the same time, pat your head with the other hand? This improves your coordination.

Another coordinating exercise. Stand with arms straight in front of you and circle one arm forwards and one arm backwards.

ground, palms down. Circle one arm slowly backwards and one arm slowly forwards at the same time so that the arms are circling in opposite directions. You may find this quite difficult, and again, practice will improve your coordination so that both arms do not try to follow the same direction.

Once you have perfected some exercises where one arm or a leg can operate independently while the other arm or leg does something different, you will find that your ability to coordinate the aids when in the saddle is greatly improved.

Relaxation

Relaxation is a state of mind that creates a physical state of ease and calmness. It is something that some people find very easy to achieve, while for others it is something that, like coordination, has to be worked at. Without a doubt, the more relaxed you can be when approaching anything to do with the horse, the easier will be your rapport and harmony with him. Horses do not understand our moods, tensions and anxieties. To maximise your enjoyment and progress with your riding, work on developing a state of relaxation before going for your lesson.

You will probably find that you have a less than fulfilling riding session if you arrive at your lesson:

- Late, because you set out from home too late and then got stuck in traffic.

- Stressed, because you argued with your husband/wife/mother etc. before dashing out.

- Clock watching, because, for example, straight after the lesson you have to go shopping before picking the kids up from school.

The stresses and tensions that you bring with you as you mount the horse will probably impede some of your progress within the lesson. It is useful to clear your mind of everything that is not relevant to your riding lesson, then your maximum effort and attention can be focused on your riding.

Relaxation is something that you can practise and develop at home. The following simple exercises will help you to relax and develop your skill at being able to relax whenever you want.

- Teach yourself to breathe deeply and slowly. Using your whole chest and upper body, feel your lungs expand and your diaphragm stretch to allow maximum intake of air; fill your lungs more deeply and fully than you usually do. Expel the air slowly and in a controlled way, not allowing a sudden rush of air from out of your lungs.

- Close your eyes (in a safe situation – not while driving the car!) and imagine yourself in a place where you would feel totally at ease and calm (perhaps lying on a sun-kissed beach in the tropics). Concentrate on eliminating all the crowding problems of the day and think only of your idyllic situation. Feel the relaxation permeate every part of your body.

Use simple relaxation exercises on a regular basis so that it becomes easy for you to achieve a calm state of mind, irrespective of the stresses around you. This skill can be hugely useful in all walks of life **as well** as in your riding.

Read and learn

While this book is your gateway to learning to ride, you may wish to seek further knowledge through the written word. These days there are many books and magazines on the market for enthusiastic would-be riders, people who own horses and those who wish to compete in the various disciplines. So what else can you read?

More stretching, through yoga. (Photo taken from from **Yoga for Equestrians**, by Linda Benedik and Veronica Wirth, published by Kenilworth Press)

■ Monthly publications such as *Your Horse*, *Horse and Rider* and *Horse* magazine provide interesting articles and information for the horse enthusiast and the amateur owner and rider. There are often true stories from riders who have experienced unusual situations with their horses, articles by well-known and successful competitive riders and training sections to educate readers.

■ The weekly magazine that most serious competitive riders and professional 'horse' people read is *Horse and Hound*, and this too can provide interesting articles and advertisements for holiday courses and lecture demonstrations with riders of national or international reputation. If you find one of these in your dentist's waiting room then it will provide you with some useful reading.

■ Many top riders in eventing, dressage and show jumping have written books of their own personal experiences and about the horses they have trained and taken to success. These books provide an interesting insight into the commitment required to achieve the pinnacle of success in equestrian sport and often give enjoyable accounts of the rocky path to achievement. ('Horsey' books can be purchased through the British Horse Society Bookshop – whose details are given at the back of the book. They have a comprehensive book list and members of the BHS receive a discount on purchases.)

Learning from reading can only be part of the picture. That knowledge must then be put into practice. It can, however, greatly enhance your practical 'hands on' learning if you understand the theory behind what you are trying to do.

What to watch

Anything involving horses will be interesting to the beginner rider who is developing a passion for equines. Just where do you look?

A 'FREE' RIDE? A WORD OF CAUTION FOR NOVICE RIDERS

Some time after you have started taking riding lessons, you may be offered the chance to ride a horse belonging to a friend or acquaintance. At face value, it seems a generous offer and an opportunity to have a 'free' ride, but a word of caution if you are a novice rider:

- Your friend (it may be a close friend or one not so well known to you) has little or no knowledge of your experience (even if you tell them how much or little you have done).

- Your friend's horse may have been ridden solely by his owner and never by a relatively inexperienced rider. Horses that you ride in a riding school are well used to carrying beginner riders and 'putting up with' the unclear and uncoordinated aids that may or may not be forthcoming from their riders.

- Your instructor is trained to recognise when you are nervous/verging on losing control/unable to manage the situation; your friend, however, is unlikely to have this ability unless he/she has taught novice riders.

- There may be no suitably confined area in which you may have a safe, controlled ride. If you had never driven a car before or were of limited experience, would you go onto a motorway in a friend's fast car and 'have a go'? I hope not! Nor would you jump into the deep end of the swimming pool having only had a couple of lessons in the shallow end of the pool.

School horses are very special horses: they learn to 'help' their beginner riders, who may not be able to help themselves. Your instructor will also have expertise in ensuring that your early lessons are both safe and progressive.

By all means visit your friend and get involved with his/her horse(s), but be careful about 'having a ride' unless you are pretty sure that the horse is safe, sensible and used to inexperienced riders, and that your friend fully understands your limited ability and will not 'push you into deep water'. (There's more about riding privately owned horses in Chapter 11.)

- If you have time to stay at the riding school you could either watch the next lesson after yours, or arrive early and watch the lesson before. So much can be learned by watching other riders and familiarising yourself with the terms used during a lesson.

- If your area or town has a local newspaper, look in the advertisements for 'what's on'. Here you should find notices of local competitions, horse shows,

Milling around in the collecting ring at a local show. (Be careful that you do not get into a position where you, or your horse, could get kicked – as in the case of the rider in the striped shirt who is perilously close to the back of a grazing horse whose owner is chatting and unaware.)

or pleasure rides; this information can also often be found in local tack shops or feed merchants. If you want to watch a small competition, just take yourself along. This can be hugely educational – for one thing, you will realise that not everyone who owns a horse rides brilliantly. Small local competitions can be great fun for the amateur owner/rider and you can watch most, if not all, of the working in (warming up) and the actual competition. Major competitions like Badminton or Burghley Horse Trials, the Horse of the Year Show or Olympia are exciting to attend and give a feeling for the dedication required to achieve elite performance status. Watching top riders in action is very motivating.

■ Find out if there is a local riding club in your area (another reason for joining the BHS, because most British riding clubs are affiliated to the BHS, who can give you a full list of clubs throughout the UK). Riding clubs welcome mounted and unmounted riders at club activities. Unmounted members will usually pay a much reduced membership fee but can join in club activities. As a non-riding member you can be very useful, perhaps as a writer for dressage judges, a steward for classes, scorer, or a secretary for entries. You can learn a great deal from your involvement and have a lot of fun meeting like-minded people into the bargain.

■ If you just love to watch horses, then racing (flat and steeplechase) may also interest you. You may have a racecourse reasonably near to home, otherwise there is usually racing on television at least at the weekend and often during the week as well.

The above list will ensure that if you truly begin to indulge your love of seeing, breathing and 'living' horses then you will never be at home. I take no responsibility for leading you astray and showing you how to further enjoy your passion for horses other than through your once-a-week ride!

Summary

Learn as much as you can by reading, watching and 'being around horses' with someone of experience there to help you with awareness and handling of the horse in the 'real' situation. Come to each lesson with a positive and enthusiastic approach to getting as much from the lesson as you can. Remember that teaching is a two-way thing. You can only learn effectively by recognising the effort made by your instructor to impart knowledge to you, working to reciprocate that effort with the energy you put in to receiving the information, and acting on it.

chapter 6

Making progress in your lessons

Every lesson will follow the basic plan that we have already discussed:

- Meeting the horse you are to ride.

- Leading your horse out to the arena where you will ride.

- Mounting and preparing to ride (adjusting girth and stirrups).

- Moving off and beginning to work.

As already discussed, the early lessons will either be on the lunge rein or on the lead rein, but nevertheless the work will almost certainly involve some work without stirrups.

Working without stirrups

This is a method of riding which is renowned for developing the rider's depth and security of the seat **but** the way it is used, particularly for novice riders, is critical in achieving the required effect. Long periods without stirrups can be tiring, and this creates tension in the rider which is then counterproductive.

When you first work without stirrups you should be shown exactly what to do with your stirrup leathers and irons.

- The buckle at the top of the stirrup leather should be pulled away from the stirrup bar so that the leather can then be laid across the horse's wither. This prevents the buckle from interfering with the thigh of the rider's leg. Both leathers should be adjusted in this way.

- The offside leather should be crossed over the horse's neck. The nearside (left) stirrup is then laid over the offside one. This sequence of crossing enables the rider (if for any reason he has dismounted, voluntarily or otherwise!) to be able to drop down the left stirrup to use for remounting.

- The stirrup leathers should always lie on the horse's neck, not on the saddle

Stirrup leathers snugly and safely crossed over the withers so that the rider can work comfortably without stirrups.

The rider showing a good position without stirrups. Working without stirrups will help to make your position deeper and more secure.

where they could be in the way of the rider.

- When the stirrups are replaced for use, the buckle should be pulled snugly up to the stirrup bar again and the irons slipped carefully down the side of the horse so that they do not bang the horse's side or the rider's ankle.

- Lastly, the rider should 'feel' for the stirrups and avoid looking down and handling the stirrup iron onto their foot.

Your first experience of work without stirrups should be at the halt, probably for a few suppling exercises at the end of your first lesson. The next occasion may involve some work without stirrups in walk, and later the trot will be introduced.

Every time you work without stirrups, it should help to deepen your position in the saddle, make you more independent as a rider, more supple and confident and altogether a better rider. However, these developments will only occur if:

- Every time you quit and cross your stirrups, your instructor (and in due course **you**) makes a point of reassessing your basic position. Make it a habit mentally to check your position and make minor corrections yourself. If there are mirrors in the arena in which you ride, then use them to check your alignment. In the early lessons your instructor should be helping you constantly to maintain a good position; he/she should correct any small faults that creep in and make suggestions that will help you not to lose your correct basic position.

- To be able to feel comfortable in the centre of the saddle you must be able to relax. **Relaxation** is of paramount importance for the rider – if you are tense and stiff you will not be flexible enough to move with the horse and stay in harmony with him.

- **Good breathing technique** helps relaxation, which in turn helps maintain a good position.

If you feel confident and comfortable in the work without stirrups then it can help your riding tremendously, probably more than any other single aspect of work on a horse.

When you work without stirrups try and 'feel' the movement of the horse under you. Within your basic position there should be a feeling of elasticity throughout your body, so that you are able to move 'with' the horse. This elasticity should be particularly felt in the small of your back. There is a natural tendency when you first work without stirrups to try to 'hold' yourself in place on the saddle, particularly in the trot, which can feel quite bouncy. This 'holding' usually manifests itself in the following ways:

- **Gripping with the knees** – this pushes you up off the saddle and in fact makes you more insecure (then you grip more and a vicious circle is established).

- **Tightening in the shoulders** and taking a stronger or unsteady contact on the reins – this can cause some loss of harmony with the horse and a general lack of balance in the rider.

- **Tension** – this can lead to a loss of balance and the seat slipping from side to side, and you may end up clutching at the front of the saddle or hanging on to the reins in an effort to maintain balance and position.

It is your instructor's responsibility to monitor carefully:

- How much work you do without stirrups in each lesson and how you cope with the physical demands of the work.

- How much of that work is in trot, moving in and out of trot, and when you are capable of making these changes of pace without holding on to the saddle.

- How comfortable and confident you feel about work without stirrups.

Above all, work without stirrups should develop the independence of your seat, i.e. your ability to coordinate your aids on the horse without relying on the reins for your balance and maintenance of position.

Hands

Your hands are an integral part of your overall position and therefore your balance and coordination. The novice rider's hands are frequently referred to by the instructor, with comments such as:

- 'The horse's mouth is very sensitive, so you mustn't pull.'

- 'Keep your hands very light; don't pull on the reins.'

- 'Give with your hands; don't pull back.'

- 'Never pull back on the horse's mouth.'

While all these comments are absolutely valid, the fact that the horse's mouth is fragile and vulnerable can become a focus for the beginner. The result is that some beginner riders become oversensitised to the horse's mouth and then fail to be positive enough about managing their balance and position sufficiently to enable them to coordinate all the aids (seat, legs, hands and, where necessary, voice).

The beginner rider will obviously lack balance and security in the early stages. As a result some uncoordinated movements may cause the reins to be used in a sharp or sometimes rough way, which may be less than comfortable for the horse. It is the instructor's responsibility to:

- Work consistently within the lesson structure to improve the rider's balance, depth of position and therefore coordination so that the rein aids are given with as much harmony as the rider can muster.

- Choose work that is within the scope of the novice rider so that the timing and application of the aids may be as harmonious as possible.

- Make the rider aware of any rough or hurried actions with the reins which perhaps could have been avoided with more thought and preparation.

The above policy will ensure that you develop a 'feel' for the comfort of the horse as a result of improving your own depth and security and therefore your riding ability and effect. The better your seat and security, the more independent your hands will become because there is no reliance on the reins for balance to stay in the saddle. It is your instructor's responsibility to guide your lessons to this overall aim. It is your responsibility to aim for as much depth and security in your position as you can and to strive to develop hands which can control and regulate the horse confidently and competently through clear rein aids, because you have achieved good balance.

Learning about trot diagonals

As you already know, the trot is a two-time gait. The horse's legs move in diagonal pairs, and between each beat there is a 'moment of suspension' when all four legs are off the ground and the horse is 'in the air'. It is this lift off the ground which gives the trot the bounce that you have utilised in rising to the trot.

It stands to reason, therefore, that you will be rising when one diagonal pair of legs is on the ground, and sitting when the other pair of legs is on the ground.

Knowing which pair of legs is on the ground when you are sitting or rising means that you can recognise which diagonal you are riding on.

The diagonal pairs of legs are named from the front legs. Therefore the **left diagonal** is:

- the left front leg with the right hind leg;

and the **right diagonal** is:

- the right front leg with the left hind leg

Recognising which diagonal you are riding on and 'changing the diagonal' will be part of your early lessons. But, you may ask, why is it useful to be able to recognise and change diagonal?

- If you habitually 'sit' on one diagonal, the horse's muscles will not be used evenly. He will be stronger on the 'sit' side because he is carrying your weight as you sit. Although he is still carrying your weight on the side that you always 'rise', it is distributed differently and his muscles will therefore develop slightly differently, so making the horse less even on both sides.

- A well-schooled horse should feel the same in his work on both reins (left or right). One of the ways this is achieved is by riding him equally on both diagonals in trot (so his muscles are developed evenly).

- Using both diagonals equally, helps to further develop your 'feel' and coordination and your dexterity at being as competent on one rein (in one direction) as you are on the other.

- Regular change of the diagonal as you change the rein will ensure that the horse stays as supple as possible on both reins and therefore a more comfortable ride.

When should you start to learn about diagonals?

- When you can maintain a consistent rhythm in rising trot.

- When you can move quite smoothly from walk to sitting trot, to rising trot, back to sitting trot and back to walk again while maintaining a fairly balanced position.

- When you can make the transitions described above and keep looking forward, with your hands steady and not seeking support on the front of the saddle.

Learning about diagonals is usually quite easy for most people, although others find the concept more difficult, particularly those who have difficulty in telling left from right or those with any degree of

Learning to ride 'outside' the arena or school further develops your skill and enjoyment.

dyslexia. If you fall into one of these categories, then don't worry about it, especially if your class-mates appear to be grasping the lesson very easily. It is not a big problem and will in no way prevent you from furthering your enjoyment of riding or your development as a rider. Learning about diagonals is important, but you may find that it is something that comes to you as your overall competence improves and your natural 'feel' becomes more identifiable.

The following system should help you to understand the concept of diagonals in trot and should enhance the teaching that you receive during your riding lessons. Remember that anything you 'learn' in theory from this or any other book should be well practised at any opportunity when you ride so that the lesson becomes a truly practical skill.

As previously stated, always adjust your position before you start trying anything new, then readjust to correct any faults which may have crept in during the work.

First, in walk, try the following exercise:

- Keep an active forward-going walk as your priority. Glance down at the horse's shoulders in front of you (do not allow your upper body to tip forward; stay on your seat, maintaining a good position and just allow your eyes to look down).

- You should see the horse's shoulders immediately in front of your knees either side of the withers. Watch each shoulder in turn – as the shoulder moves forward, the horse's foot is off the ground; as the shoulder moves back towards you, the horse's foot is on the ground.

- Say out loud (or to yourself if more appropriate) 'now' every time one shoulder (left or right, it doesn't matter) moves back towards you.

- If you can do this in walk it will give you the idea of what you will try to do in trot (where everything happens faster and with more bounce!). Your instructor should help you to adjust your voice-timing if you are not in sync with the leg.

- Next, try the same exercise in trot. Now suddenly you have to prioritise! You have several things to think about all at the same time and this will strain your ability. Something may be lost – balance, position, control of the horse.

- You must try to concentrate on one thing at a time. So, make the transition to sitting trot, then take rising trot and, only when you have a good rhythm in your rising, see if you can glance at the shoulder (choose just one at a time).

- In trot you need to decide which shoulder is coming back towards you as you sit in the saddle. Glance at each shoulder in turn and try to say 'now' every time you see the shoulder move back. You should find that you are sitting in the saddle in time with one of your 'nows'.

- Whichever shoulder is moving back as you sit, is the diagonal you are riding on. If the left shoulder is moving back as you sit, you are on the left diagonal; if it is the right shoulder, you are on the right diagonal.

In the first few lessons your aim should be to practise identifying which shoulder is coming back as you sit. You should find that it is as often the left as it is

RIDING SCHOOL TERMINOLOGY

The following commands will become increasingly familiar during your lessons:

- **'Prepare to . . .'** Primes you to correct your position and think of the aids that you will use to carry out whatever action is asked.

- **'The whole ride . . .'** This means everyone at the same time.

- **'One at a time or in succession . . .'** Means individually.

- **'Quit and cross your stirrups'** This means take your feet out of your stirrup irons and cross your stirrup leathers (and irons) over your horse's neck so that you can ride comfortably without your stirrups.

- **'Change the rein'** This means make a change of direction from left to right or right to left. In the early stages of your lessons your instructor will explain how to change the rein. Later on you may begin to choose for yourself.

- **'Go large'** Use the whole school, going around the outside track.

- **'Make much'** Make a fuss of your horse (pat him) when he has gone well.

The following terms refer to some of the shapes (also known as figures) that you will be asked to ride. They are shown in the accompanying diagrams:

- **Circle** Circles can be of various size, starting with a 20m circle and progressing through 15m to 10m, and in some cases (usually only in walk) down to about 5m. (The diagrams show where these can be ridden in a 20m x 40m school.)

- **Serpentine** A snaking figure, usually of three loops but can be more.

- **Loop** Usually 5m or 10m.

If during your lessons a term comes up which is unclear to you, you must ask for an explanation. Do not be embarrassed about asking.

the right. Sometimes, however, you find that it is more frequently one diagonal. This may mean that the horse is a bit one-sided and always puts you onto the diagonal he likes to carry you on. Or it may mean that you, as a rider, favour one side over the other. Unless I think about it, I find that I always favour the left diagonal.

How to change diagonal

When you are entirely happy about recognising which diagonal you are on then you can think about being able to change from one diagonal to the other. This is very easy:

- **Just sit in the saddle for one extra beat and your next rise will put you on the opposite diagonal to the one you started on**.

Your sequence of rising would therefore be: up, down, up, down, up, down, **down**, up. By sitting for a second 'down' beat you automatically change the sequence of your rising trot onto the opposite diagonal.

Like learning the initial sequence of rising trot, once you can control your seat to sit for that one extra beat, you will find changing the diagonal the easiest of movements.

By this stage your instructor should have discussed when the diagonal is changed: quite simply, whenever you are in rising trot and you make a change of rein, the diagonal should be changed.

It is normal practice to ride on the outside diagonal, i.e. if on the left rein you ride on the right diagonal (outside to the way the horse is bent), and on the left rein you ride on the right diagonal.

Developing the work on diagonals

Once you have understood the basic concept of the use of diagonals in trot then this becomes another facet of your knowledge as a rider, but do make sure that you don't over-concentrate on this one aspect. Like any new-found skill there is a period of time where you have to think hard about what you are trying to do, and then gradually, through practice, the skill becomes increasingly automatic. The use of diagonals should not assume so much importance that you forget:

- To work on maintaining a good position.

- To ride forward into a trot which is rhythmical, active and sustained.

- To think about your balance and relaxation in sitting and rising trot.

It can happen that you are so busy concentrating on looking to see which diagonal you are on when you take rising trot that:

- You look down as you go into trot, which affects your position.

- Your lack of a good position affects your ability to ride the trot forward into a secure rhythm.

- Your inability to establish a forward rhythm in the trot prevents you from being able to see or establish the correct diagonal.

In time, you should find that you improve in recognising and changing diagonal, until ultimately you can feel which diagonal you are on. Some horses give you a much clearer 'feel' of the diagonal than others, so take that into account as well.

Working behind a leading file

Once you are riding independently, off the lead rein or lunge rein, you may find it easier to develop your confidence if you can 'follow' a leading file (i.e. a rider of greater experience and expertise who can provide a regular and consistent pace for you to follow). It is quite common for an instructor to have a group of fairly novice riders behind one competent leading file. While the leading file is useful as a support you must still ride positively to develop your own independence.

Your aims while riding behind a leading file should be:

- To work hard to maintain a good position.

- To control your horse so that you maintain a distance of between half and one horse's length between you and the horse in front.

- To work on applying well-prepared aids so that your horse listens to you and does not just follow the horse in front.

- To think for yourself and make sure that at any time you could go forward more to close a developing gap or stop if the horse in front stops.

Simple school figures

We will now consider some of the basic school figures that you will ride very regularly through your riding career. As with the use of diagonals the more you ride these figures, the more familiar they will become to you and the more accurately you will be able to ride them. However, before embarking on the figures we need to recap on how the aids will allow you to ride them.

Very simply, the rider's basic aids for controlling the horse are a coordination of the following:

- The inside leg creates the energy and forward movement of the horse. It is usually positioned 'on the girth'.

- The outside leg supports the job of creating forward movement but when also positioned a little behind the girth it controls the hindquarters of the

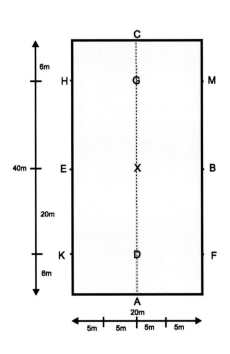

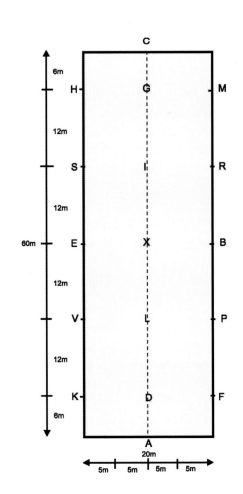

ABOVE Standard size arena.
RIGHT International size arena.

Various ways to change the rein.

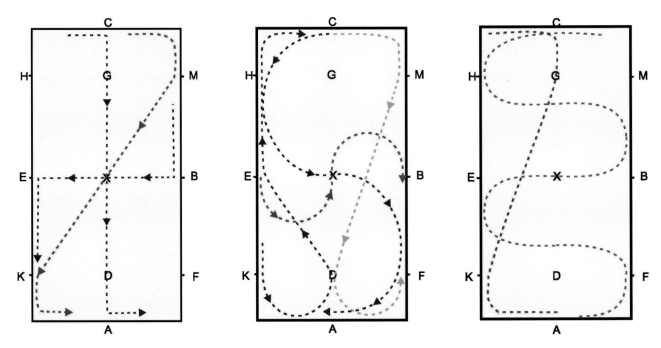

'INSIDE' AND 'OUTSIDE' EXPLAINED

When discussing **inside** and **outside** it is important to understand that these terms **always** relate to the way the horse is bending, never to the arena. In other words if the horse is bending to the right then the inside leg and inside rein are those on the right side, and the outside leg and rein are those on the left. If you were riding around the arena on the left rein with the horse bent to the right then the right leg and rein would still be the inside leg and rein.

horse and prevents them from swinging outwards.

■ The inside rein creates a little flexion in the direction of travel. There should be just enough bend to be able just to see the horse's eyelid on that side.

■ The outside rein controls the flexion (by not allowing too much bend in the neck) and also controls the speed of the horse.

These aids, applied variously in coordinating sequences, control virtually everything that you will ever ride with the horse, from a simple circle in walk or rising trot to an advanced dressage movement such as a canter pirouette.

We will now describe the aids and method of riding a **20m circle, a turn** and a **serpentine of three loops**. Whether executed in walk or trot the method and aids are the same, only the gait is different.

Circles, loops and serpentines.

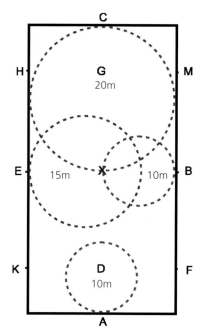
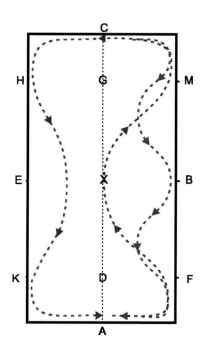
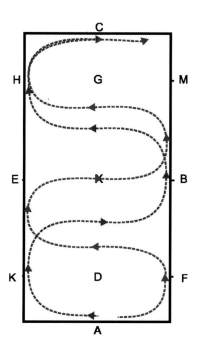

OUTSIDE HAND controls the pace and regulates the bend

INSIDE HAND creates direction and bend

Riding a circle. The bend of the horse is clear and should be maintained continuously for the duration of the circle.

INSIDE LEG creates and maintains impulsion

OUTSIDE LEG, placed slightly behind the girth, helps to prevent the quarters swinging

A 20m circle

When riding a circle of 20m it is easier to judge the exact shape and size of the circle if ridden from A or C, rather than from E or B, which requires a little more skill.

Let's assume you're riding a 20m circle from A:

- Ride a good corner preceding the start of the circle.

- From A maintain active, forward steps with both legs but with the outside leg behind the girth to control the quarters as you start the circle.

- The inside rein creates a little direction to guide the horse onto the curve of the circle and sustain the circle line.

- The outside rein controls the pace and regulates the bend on the circle.

- On completing the continuous curve of the circle, the outside rein straightens the horse as you ride forward with an active inside leg to direct the horse onto a straight line away from the circle and into the next corner.

A turn

The aids for a turn are exactly the same as the aids for a circle, the only difference being that:

- They will be applied for a shorter time – only for three or four strides – for the duration of the turn itself.

- The inside rein may need to ask far more decisively than on the circle actually to cause the horse to make a change of direction through 45° or 90° rather than the more gentle curve of a large circle.

- The more decisive turn will therefore need more positive support with both legs.

- A steady contact in the outside rein will ensure that the horse maintains balance and smoothness through the turn.

- The horse must look in the direction in which he is turning.

A three-loop serpentine

This is a series of changes of direction through smooth half circles of a little over 10m diameter. (See illustration, page 81.)

The rider needs first to plan where the movement will be ridden through the school. (See use of cones, page 85.)

- The first loop is ridden with the same aids as for the circle.

- The aids are reversed over the centre line and reapplied in the new direction.

- Similarly into the final loop, the aids are smoothly reversed again.

This movement develops coordination and suppleness in both horse and rider.

Understanding transitions

As you already know, transitions are changes of gait or pace, from one gait to another, e.g. from walk to trot, or from trot to canter. However, they can also refer to a change of pace **within** a gait. In your early riding experience this will feel like 'going faster' and 'going slower' within the pace, e.g. trot.

As your knowledge and experience expands, you will come to understand that there are several variations within the gaits, notably collection and extension (although there are also 'working', 'medium', and 'free' versions). When a horse is collected his strides become shorter and higher, and he works in a wonderful state of energy, with a slow rhythm and powerful steps. When he lengthens his strides to the utmost, powering along with ground-covering, elastic strides but still with the same rhythm and tempo, he is working in extension. Learning how to produce and ride these paces is something to look forward to for the future. For now, back to the more straightforward transitions.

Transitions require:

- **Preparation**. The better the preparation, the smoother the transition is likely to be.

- **Forwardness**. Whether the transition is upward (e.g. from walk to trot) or downward (e.g. from trot to walk) the movement must be **forward**. There should always be a feeling that the horse is ridden from the leg to the hand, never the other way around.

- **Clear aid application**. Apply hand and leg aids as clearly as you can.

- **'Feel'** for what the horse is doing underneath you and therefore as much harmony between you and the horse as possible. Transitions must never be rough.

Taking each of these points in a little more detail.

Preparation

When thinking about carrying out a transition your instructor should remind you to:

- Correct your position. Think about sitting as well as you can so that the aids you give for the transition will be applied as clearly as possible.

- Think about the aids that you are going to give, and if necessary shorten your reins so that you will be able to apply smooth rein aids effectively.

- Think about the pace you are already in and make sure that it is forward and rhythmical to the best of your ability.

Forwardness

The pace must be going forward because to make any transition the horse must have active hind legs, powering underneath him and assisting in balancing his weight and yours. He will then be able to change pace smoothly.

As a novice rider it is easy to find that as you prepare to make the transition your preparation itself becomes a trigger for anticipation by the horse. He sneakily quickens or slows down before you ask him to make the change of pace. This may seem very helpful because you were aiming for the transition anyway, but you must avoid it becoming a habit. If you consistently allow the horse to make the decisions, then you are not really 'riding' him: he is in control. In this situation you no longer have authority, and this is a slippery slope to embark upon. As you prepare, concentrate on the forwardness and control it. If there is too much forwardness before making a transition, say, from trot to canter, then regulate it through a positive position and some steadying aids on the reins. If there is not enough and the horse slows down in readiness for a downward transition, then positively use your legs to maintain the pace before giving the aid to change pace.

Clear aid application

Think through the aids that you will be aiming to give.

In an upward transition you want to:

- Maintain a good position.

- Actively use both legs on the horse's side (your inside leg a little more on the girth and the outside leg a little more behind the girth) to encourage him forward.

■ Maintain an elastic contact on the reins, with the reins short enough to influence the horse.

■ Allow a fluent increase in pace via your hands as you move up to the next pace.

In a downward transition:

■ Your hands prevent the horse from continuing to progress forward in the same pace, thus compressing the energy between the legs and hands and ensuring that the horse remains elastic and balanced as he comes into the change of pace.

■ A backward pull on the reins should always be avoided, particularly if this is not supported by a positive riding position in the saddle and an ability to use your legs a little in advance of the rein aids.

'Feel'

I make no apology for mentioning 'feel' again and again throughout this book. **Riding is about feeling**; 'feel' is an intrinsic part of the development of your competence. 'Feel' is something that we all have to some degree or another. As a rider it is something that you must work on, think about and aim to develop to improve your harmony with every horse you ride.

As you gain a greater 'feel' or awareness of the horse under you, so you will develop better timing for when to apply the aids for whatever you are trying to do. In a class lesson your instructor will probably tell you exactly when to make a transition, say, to trot or walk. In your early lessons this is very helpful, because you will not have the expertise to know or to decide when to make the transition yourself. Your instructor will use his or her knowledge to pick the optimum time for you to make the change of pace. Good school horses will respond partly to your developing skills and partly to the voice and body language of your teacher – this in itself should help you to develop the right sort of 'feel'. Later on, you will increasingly be aiming for some independence in making your own decisions as to the timing of a transition, based on your own assessment of the 'feel' of the horse's way of going.

TRANSITIONS

Transitions are a basic tool of riding. Whenever you ride a horse, be it in the riding school, out hacking, competing or leisure riding, you will always be required to make changes of pace and changes of direction. These are basic tools of horsemanship.

Further control

Poles, cones and other 'props'

Here we take a look at ways in which your instructor may help you to develop your control skills by using a selection of props. The idea of using cones and poles etc. is to make your lessons more interesting, challenging and varied whilst still enabling your confidence, basic position and security to be further established before the next big step of learning to canter.

Poles and the like can be used to sharpen up the novice rider's ability to stop, start, turn left and right, and this imbues riders with an early sense of control and achievement. These two feelings go a long way to building confidence in novices, who may still be greatly in awe of the feeling of size, power and independence of the four-legged creature underneath them.

Poles

Poles can be used in the following ways to develop control in transitions, turns and steering:

Using poles can be fun and improve your control and coordination.
BELOW Halting between poles.
BELOW RIGHT Halting with the front legs on one side of the pole and the hind legs on the other.

- A pole is placed on the centre line from E to B, at X. Riders make a turn at A or C in walk (later this can be ridden in trot) and approach the pole. They aim to allow the horse to step over the pole with his front legs only, and then halt before the hind legs cross it Thus the horse will stand with his front legs on one side of the pole and his hind legs on the other.

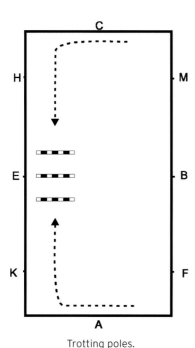

Trotting poles.

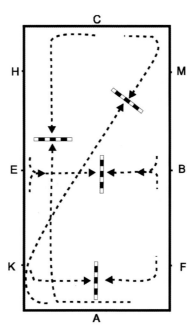

Poles at random.

This exercise involves thinking ahead, preparation, and 'feel', as well as clearly applied aids for an accurate result. Obviously, if performed in trot, the horse must first come to walk before halting over the pole, thus involving another transition within the exercise.

The pole could be placed anywhere in the school as long as the line to the pole is ridden carefully and a clear explanation of the line of approach is given by the instructor.

■ Two poles can be set out parallel to each other (almost anywhere in the school) for a rider to pass between. Riders make a turn into the mouth of the poles, followed by another after the poles. A halt transition before leaving the poles could also be part of the exercise. The poles should be placed at least 4ft (1.2m) apart so that a horse can comfortably travel between them.

■ Several poles can be placed at random around the school and riders asked to take their own line (individually) over the centre of each pole and perhaps link two or more poles together.

Cones

Small or large cones are very useful as 'props' for improving control and steering. They can be used in various ways but the following are probably the most common:

■ For bending (usually on the centre line). The rider has to bend the horse in and out of a line of cones, and pass around the top cone before riding the horse back through the cones to the start.

Cones for bending direction lines. More cones could be used in a 20m x 60m school. Fewer cones make the exercise easier.

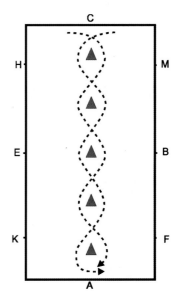

■ For improving the ability of the rider to execute good corners. A cone may be placed either near to the corner to ride around, or in the corner to help the rider to ride more accurately 'into' the corner.

Other props

Other props, such as a mounting block in the corner of the school, can be used during a lesson – in this case to practise mounting and dismounting.

Some establishments put coloured markers or circles on the wall in addition to the standard letters. These marks can be helpful in learning to ride better school figures.

chapter 7

The jumping or half-seat position

You may by wondering why the jumping or half-seat position is covered before learning to canter? As an instructor of beginner and novice riders for some thirty years, I believe that riders should be given the opportunity to develop and extend their skills further in trot before they embark on canter. This encourages greater confidence, security and balance, all of which will help them enormously when they learn to canter. I have therefore chosen to cover this subject here.

Adopting the jumping or half-seat position

So far you have learned to sit in one basic riding position. In due course, as a preparation for jumping (which will come some time later), it will be necessary to think about adopting another position, which will enable you to follow the movement of the horse through his take-off, flight in the air over the fence, and his landing. This second position, which for ease I will call the jumping position (although it is also known as the half seat, light seat or poised position), enables the rider to feel secure and in balance through the changing phases of the horse's jump and – equally important – allows the horse the freedom to jump unimpeded by the rider.

The jumping position is adopted as follows:

- It **may** be necessary to shorten your stirrups by one or two holes. Your instructor will advise if this is appropriate for you and will help you individually.

- Shorten your reins and incline the upper body a little forward; as you do this you will automatically feel your seat slide a little further back in the saddle.

- At the same time think about the weight going down your lower leg and into your heel.

- Your back should remain flat and your eyes up, looking forward, so that

Jumping position. Slight variation of the upper body may be appropriate as the rider develops greater feel for speed and balance of the horse to a jump.

your shoulders stay open and not rounded.

- Your weight is now distributed between your stirrups and the saddle.

- Gradually, through 'feel', and later when you actually start to learn to jump, you will find that the amount of weight in the saddle and the stirrups will vary, depending on what you are doing. Sometimes there may be 30% in your legs and 70% in your seat; at another time there may be 50% in each. At no time, however, should there be 100% weight in either your stirrups or in your seat.

- As your 'feel' and balance develop in the use of the jumping position you will become more familiar and comfortable with it.

The rider on this grey horse shows a good basic 'jumping position'.

Standing up in the stirrups in trot and canter helps the rider develop balance over the lower leg; this in turn makes their jumping position more secure.

Using the jumping position on the flat

Once you have practised the jumping position at halt and you understand the basic concept of the position, it should then be worked on in walk. Practise moving smoothly from one position to the other while maintaining a forward, rhythmical walk. Maintain the basic position for a few strides, then, say, along one long side take jumping position, and retake the basic position again as you reach the next short side.

Once you can do this, then the same exercise can be tried in trot. Moving forward as usual from walk into sitting trot and then into rising trot, take jumping position along one long side and then retake basic position again on the short side.

Rising or sitting trot can be ridden in the jumping position in exactly the same way as you would ride them in your basic position. You can practise taking jumping position at any point around the school while riding any of the school movements you may have learned. In fact, you can practise your jumping position in any of the work we have previously discussed (e.g. using cones and poles for steering and direction).

Jumping position over trotting poles

Once you are familiar with moving into and out of jumping position and it is as easy to you as moving from rising to sitting trot or working without stirrups, then there is no reason why you cannot be taught how to negotiate trotting poles.

Trotting poles are often associated with preparing to jump but they can also be used extensively with no relation whatsoever to subsequent jumping. Here we will discuss the value of using trotting poles as an exercise to develop interest, scope and versatility in the novice rider's repertoire.

ABOVE Jumping position over a single pole, and **ABOVE RIGHT** through trotting poles.

Poles used for trotting over are usually set at approximately 4ft 6ins (1.4m) or 9ft (2.9m) apart. Poles set at 9ft (2.9m) distance are a little easier for novice riders to negotiate since they do not appear so daunting to ride towards.

If set at **4ft 6ins (1.4m)** distance the horse will place **one foot** in between each pole. At **9ft (2.9m)** distance the horse will take **one step** between each pole.

The basic principle of riding towards any pole is to:

- Ride a good line of approach and departure to and from the pole(s).
- Approach on a straight line at right angles to and in the centre of the first pole.
- Maintain a good rhythm and forwardness in the trot.
- Maintain the same speed or tempo of trot through the approach, over the pole(s) and in the departure from the pole(s).

In the early stages a single pole is set down, and then three or four poles may be used in a line. Two or more lines can be set out in different parts of the school.

The poles can be ridden over in rising-trot jumping position or sitting-trot jumping position.

As you negotiate the poles you will learn to feel and follow the increased lift or elevation in the horse's trot stride as he negotiates the poles, and this in turn will improve your balance and coordination.

Learning to canter, and riding in open order

chapter 8

The first canter

The first canter lesson is, for many, a milestone in learning to ride. It is definitely time for you to start work on learning to canter if:

- Your position in the saddle is well established.

- You are well practised in riding basic transitions, turns, circles and simple school figures.

- You have worked steadily each time you ride without your stirrups.

- You feel confident in your understanding of what you are trying to do on the horse.

- You feel increasingly positive about your control.

- You are keen to try more.

The timing of your first canter is a very individual thing, rather like coming off the lunge or lead rein. It should be personal to you and you only. This is where the organisation of a class lesson of novice riders is so vital. The instructor should be able to structure the lesson in such a way that those who are ready to canter can have their first experience of the gait, while those whose development or confidence is not quite at that level can continue other work easily in trot, without one group feeling disadvantaged by the other.

The good novice rider's horse will go easily from trot into a smooth unhurried canter and back into trot almost automatically and certainly from the voice or body language of the instructor. While the rider **must** receive the relevant knowledge to make the transition, the change of pace must be easily achieved by an inexperienced rider. We will therefore consider below what you need to know to prepare for your first experience of canter.

Canter is the third of the horse's four true gaits (walk, trot and gallop being the

RIDING IN CANTER

Canter work is **always** introduced individually; you will not be required to canter as a group!

other three). It is a faster gait than trot, but slower than gallop. (In training the horse and in competing in 'dressage', only walk, trot and canter are considered.)

Whereas walk is a four-time gait – each foot coming to the ground independently of the other three to give four clear beats – and trot is a two-time gait, with the legs moving in diagonal pairs, canter is a three-time gait, which makes it an asymmetric gait.

If you watch a horse cantering around an arena or school, you may notice that his inside foreleg (the one nearest to you) appears to take a longer step forward than his outside foreleg. If the right foreleg appears to be reaching out more, he is said to be on the 'right leg'; if the left foreleg is more prominent, he is on the 'left leg'. The sequence of the horse's legs in canter is important and is discussed in the next section.

The horse must be going forward in an active, rhythmical trot so that he has enough energy to take him into the next pace.

The rider must prepare for the transition into canter (just as with other transitions that you have practised). This involves making sure that your position is as good as possible and that you think about the aids that you need to apply.

Canter on a named leg

The sequence of the horse's legs in canter is a little more complex than that in walk and trot because it is an asymmetric pace. Naturally the horse will always balance himself, and when cantering around a curve or a corner the easiest way for him to do this is to use his legs in the following sequence:

■ The canter starts with the **outside hind leg**.

■ The diagonal pair of the **inside hind and the outside foreleg** then work together.

The rider in canter. The bandages of the horse show clearly that he is in 'left lead canter': the right hind has just finished its step, the diagonal pair (left hind and right fore) are on the ground and the left fore (leading leg) is about to strike the floor. The rider has slightly left her right shoulder behind and needs to 'follow' the horse's shoulders more.

- The last leg in the three-beat sequence is the **inside foreleg**.

Remember: 'inside' and 'outside' apply to the direction of the bend of the horse **not** to the direction of riding in the school.

In your lessons your instructor may say that the horse is 'on the wrong lead', or that you are 'on the wrong leg'. This means that the horse is not in his natural balance, and because he is taking the wrong sequence of legs he cannot produce a balanced and smooth ride. In due course, as your ability progresses, it will become increasingly important for you to influence the horse through the timing of your aids so that he 'strikes off' with the correct sequence of legs. In the early stages of learning, however, you should be riding a horse that will easily and willingly carry you forward from trot into canter with the minimum of effort on your part, other than the basic aid application.

The aids for canter

The aids that you need to learn for giving the message to the horse to ask for canter are:

- **Inside leg**, on the girth (normal position), increases pressure to ask for more forward movement.

- **Outside leg**, a little behind the girth, also increases pressure to assist in forward movement, but at the moment that you want the horse to move from trot into canter, the outside leg gives a definite press/tap/kick actually to tell the horse that that is the moment you want him to change gait.

- **Inside rein** maintains a light feeling to keep a little flexion to the inside.

- **Outside rein** regulates the speed and prevents the horse from bending too much in the neck or from increasing the trot pace.

When the horse feels the coordination of the four aids together he should move easily from trot into canter.

In the return from canter to trot, always

- prepare by thinking about your balance and position;

- grow a little taller in your upper body;

- make sure your reins are short enough;

- try to maintain a little depth and security into your seat; and then

- ease back with both reins to ask the horse to slow down.

Often the first few trot strides as you return to trot feel quite bouncy and strong. It is usually easier to go into rising trot at this stage as you will find the strength of the trot difficult to 'sit' easily to. As your competence develops so will your depth and relaxation and then you will gradually find that you can return to 'sitting' trot from canter, and this should be your aim eventually.

As your practice of the canter develops and you become more confident about progressing into and out of canter, then you can begin to think a little more about the finer points of riding the canter competently.

Preparation for canter

- The trot should be forward and rhythmical.

- You should correct your position and think of the aids you will apply.

- You should take sitting trot for a few strides before the canter strike-off, as this will enable you ultimately to sit in a better balance and therefore apply clearer aids.

- The easiest place to attempt the canter transition is as the horse enters a corner, because at this point the horse will be naturally balanced towards giving the rider the correct strike-off.

- You apply the aids for canter.

Sitting to the canter

Learning to 'sit' to the canter is the next consideration. The feeling of 'sitting' to the canter is slightly different from the feeling of 'sitting' to the trot. This is because of the basic difference between the 'bounce' in the two-time trot gait and the smoother 'rocking' of the canter gait promoted by the three-beat sequence of legs.

There are two fairly demonstrative and easy ways to describe the way the novice rider should learn to 'sit' to the canter. I hope that one or both of these may help you to master the necessary technique, which ultimately takes **practice**.

1. The feeling in canter should be as if your seat is polishing the saddle from the back (cantle) towards the front (pommel), in a continuous and fluent movement with each canter stride. Your seat should feel as if it is 'sliding' across the saddle, with your hips flexible and the small of the back relaxed.

- Your shoulders need to stay back over your hips, with the upper body tall and the lower leg stretching down. Avoid any tendency to grip up with the lower leg; the aim is to stay in balance with the movement rather than 'hold on' with any part of your body to maintain position.

- Your hands should stay still relative to the horse's mouth, i.e. they should be as still as possible whilst maintaining a contact through the reins. Because he is a living animal there will be some natural movement in his head and mouth, and your hands should be able to 'follow' this subtle movement.

■ You should look up and forward, as by looking down you will cause your shoulders to become rounded and therefore affect your seat and overall depth of position.

2. Another way is to think of the movement as being similar to the feeling you have when sitting on a child's swing, but without your feet on the ground. You have to influence the swing to move forward through the action of your hips – through flexible hips and suppleness in the small of the back you can make the swing move higher and higher in the air. There is, however, no need to 'drive' with your seat; you only need to 'swing' through the hips to follow the canter.

■ The position of the rider's upper body, hands and lower legs is as described in method **1** (see opposite).

Developing 'feel' for the canter lead

Awareness of the correct canter lead, just like awareness of which diagonal you are on in trot, takes **time** and the ability to recognise it varies from rider to rider. If you glance down the horse's inside shoulder you should be able to see the horse's inside foreleg just pushing forward in front of the outside foreleg. At the same time allow yourself to 'feel' how the horse is going. Often when the horse takes the wrong lead in canter he will quickly break back to trot to re-establish a better balance for himself. Allow yourself to 'feel' the horse 'telling' you that he is uncomfortable and wanting to come back to trot. Practise looking for the canter lead without it affecting your position (you must be able to glance down with your eyes only, not tipping the whole of your body out of balance).

Always establish the canter first and practise your position in canter before worrying about which leg you are on. If the correct canter lead becomes the priority you soon forget to ride with the forwardness necessary to achieve a good balanced canter, and then you probably induce the wrong lead because of poor technique – and so a 'vicious circle' develops.

In the early work in canter it should not be your responsibility to worry about the correct lead in canter. This is a concern for your instructor and he/she

VARIETY IN LESSON WORK

The use of both the basic riding position and the jumping position can add variety and interest to your weekly lessons. Learning to ride well is achieved only by repetition of basic work in walk, trot and canter, by the constant use of changes of pace (transitions), and by the riding of school figures to instil coordination and competence in aid application. The more varied your lesson content, the more your interest will be maintained, keeping you motivated and enthusiastic.

should very gradually pass that responsibility over to you as you become more competent.

Riding in open order

In most of your lesson work thus far you will have been riding behind a leading file and developing work individually through exercises. Many exercises in group lessons are ridden either from the leading file in succession to the rear of the ride, or sometimes by the rear file (passing the ride on the inside) carrying out an exercise and then passing the ride again to take leading file. Through these activities you learn control and independence.

The next step will be to ride **solo** – on your own, without the influence of a file order in a ride. Working in 'open order' means that you find your own space and try to maintain that space while controlling your own pace and direction. Remembering that horses are herd animals and like to 'follow', you will need to assert firm aids to influence your horse to go exactly where you want him to go and not allow him to follow another horse.

   The introduction to working in open order should come towards the end of a normal class lesson. You will then be riding confidently and with control. Initially in walk, and with everyone staying on the same rein (going around in the same direction), you should be encouraged to circle away into a space and to choose your own area in which to ride.

The following points may help you to ride more effectively in open order:

Pass left to left when riding in open order.

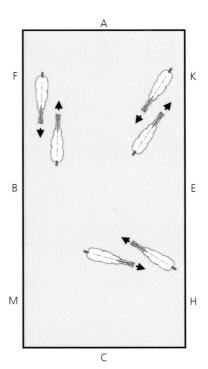

- Think ahead and plan well ahead.

- Remember that any thought you may have takes time to pass through to the horse as an action. For example, if you want the horse to make a right turn at E, you cannot give the aid as you reach E, you must be preparing at least two markers beforehand. You need to think, prepare (by correcting your position) and apply the aids, then the horse responds – all of which takes time.

- No aids should be applied sharply or without thought and preparation.

- After a change of direction or a figure remember to ride forward to regain any energy lost through the turn or figure.

- Look ahead (at least three or four markers), and be constantly thinking about where you are going and how you are going to get there. With several riders working independently, finding a clear space to ride into needs more planning than you may realise. Horses cover the ground very quickly and you'll need to have a distance of three or four markers for 'thinking time' just to stay on your intended route.

In time, your instructor should encourage you to use both walk and trot (but with everyone staying on the same rein). In addition to choosing the direction and space in which you are to ride, you will now have to designate the pace as well. Start with small bouts of trot and make a definite decision to move into trot. Trot for perhaps half a circuit of the school and then make a transition to walk again. Avoid just allowing the horse to fade out of trot and regain walk without positive influence from you. Even though you may have had it in your mind to walk, the horse knows that he made the decision and is not under your authority. It is important to make sure that any decision, however small, is yours and not the horse's!

When you can assert some basic control in open order in walk and trot then you are ready to change the rein at will. Once this situation is embarked upon then you have the following criteria to consider:

- Control of direction.

- Control of pace.

- Your location in relation to other riders who may be travelling in the opposite direction to you.

This last point requires special consideration. You must be able to:

- Think ahead (this is something you have been working on throughout your lessons).

- Prepare yourself, and therefore your horse, to avoid other horses.

- Know your left from your right, because it is an accepted system to pass other riders left hand to left hand.

Working in open order is quite demanding for inexperienced riders and should only be embarked upon for small periods of a lesson. It puts great responsibility on you as a rider – with so much to think about, you have less time to work on your position, think about the correct aid application and all the other requirements that are crowding into your head to keep you riding competently. Some horses are easier to ride in open order than others, and this again will test your ability. Riding independently, however, gives great satisfaction and should be a growing pleasure as you progress as a rider.

chapter 9

Hacking out and broadening your skills

Once you have achieved basic control of the horse in walk, trot and canter, and can stop, start, turn left and right and designate when you change direction and at what pace, it is fun and challenging to see whether that ability is transferable into the great 'outdoors'.

'Hacking' is the term used for riding out in the countryside on horseback. Hacking may be on:

- Country lanes with very little traffic.

- Busier rural lanes and roads with variable traffic, depending on the time of day.

- Bridlepaths and tracks crossing farmland.

- Forestry Commission paths within woodland.

- Commons and heathland with designated tracks.

- Moorland and hills.

Where you ride out will depend largely on the area in which you live and the type of hacking country that exists around your riding school. Some riding schools do not hack out at all, because their locale is not suitable for safe riding out. In this case you may need to seek another establishment and go hacking from there.

However, before you go tearing off to book a hack, consider the difference in riding in a wide-open unenclosed area compared to riding in the comparative safety of an arena or school. Some comparisons can be drawn between learning to swim in a swimming pool and then transferring that skill to swimming in the sea. Anyone who has experienced the feeling of swimming out of their depth for the first time, in a vast expanse of undulating seawater stretching to infinity, will know what I mean.

Your first hack

If you are interested in hacking out then discuss the possibility with your instructor. Your confidence and skill level will dictate whether you are ready to take on this challenge. You should be able to:

- Control a quiet horse in walk, trot and preferably canter.

- Feel confident that you can stop, start and turn without being dependent on the horse in front of you.

- Maintain a balanced and comfortable position in walk, trot and canter.

- Feel confident riding without stirrups in walk, trot and preferably canter. (You will not be expected to ride without your stirrups on a hack, but the fact that you could lose one or both stirrups at any time during the ride should not unduly alarm you.)

- Feel confident about maintaining an independent attitude to controlling your own horse, not always looking for instruction from your teacher.

For your first hack, you should go out in a small group with an instructor who has taught you before (assuming that it is with your regular school). Ideally you should ride a horse that you have ridden previously in your lessons, one that you feel confident and positive about and that you enjoy riding. While you may have ridden one or two more challenging horses in your lessons, for your first hack you want to be mounted on a horse well within your scope and ability.

Depending on the number in the group there will be one or more competent 'escorts'. There should be at least one instructor, but the ride may be escorted by competent riders, not necessarily trained teachers, giving support and assistance. Ideally there should be a ratio of one competent person to every four

BELOW Being able to open and close a gate while mounted is a useful skill when riding out. BELOW RIGHT A picnic ride can be great fun in the school holidays or when the weather is good.

Riding out may involve riding on the road, in which case fluorescent clothing is advisable.

riders. Having said that, it would be more difficult for an instructor to be in charge of four first-time hackers than perhaps to take out four riders comprising two who have hacked previously and two who are completely new to it.

Your first hack should take you on an easy route with well-controlled areas for changes of pace. That way you will have a thoroughly good experience of riding out and will be motivated to do it again.

As your experience broadens you will inevitably ride up and down hills and may have to negotiate gates. At first, gates will be opened and closed for you by your escort. Later, you will learn how to manage these yourself. Ridng through water may be another new experience.

If you ride on a public highway, however quiet the road or lane, it will involve meeting traffic. There are established practices for riders on the road and these can be studied in the Highway Code and the BHS booklet, *Riding and Roadcraft*. Your instructor should explain the basic rules of riding on the road before your first hack.

As a result of hacking out, your ability as an independent rider should greatly increase. Inevitably, however well controlled the hack, there will be occasions when you have to think for yourself and deal with situations as they arise. For example, if a bird flies out of a hedge causing your horse to spook (shy) and run forwards, you will have to control him and prevent him from running away in fear. You may need to reassure him with a pat on the neck and a quiet word, and quickly regain your balance and position. This is something you have to learn through trial and error as the instructor/escort may not be close enough to see your dilemma and advise you on how to cope with it.

Riding out can be such a great pleasure that some riders choose only to hack, and continue to develop their skill and competence in this type of riding. Other riders prefer to continue to strive for greater achievements in the arena or

A large group of riders trekking on moorland.

school, working on depth of position and general ability to ride, and on understanding the training of the horse. Others again are keen to progress their riding in the school to develop jumping skills. (See next chapter.)

Other opportunities to broaden your skills

As your confidence and ability grow you may feel positive enough to consider other opportunities to ride. These could arise if:

- You have the chance to ride while away on holiday.

- A friend owns a horse and offers you a ride on it.

You may also wish to add to your horse knowledge by learning about stable management and horse care.

Riding on the beach can be a wonderful experience both for horse and rider.

Riding holidays

Riding holidays can be taken both at home or abroad and the opportunities are extensive and expanding all the time. My advice is: research the holiday well before you commit yourself. If you can, seek personal recommendation from someone whose opinion you value.

What you should find out about a possible riding holiday:

- How long will you spend in the saddle each day? (It may be as much as six hours per day for five or more days running, which you may find extremely gruelling if you have ridden for only an hour a week for a few months.)

- What type of terrain will you be riding over? Smooth, flat, grassy plains may

Trail riding, Western style, in Arizona.

involve a lot of riding in faster paces; steep mountain tracks will be tackled mostly in walk and may involve getting off and leading the horse in hand.

- How many will there be in the group, and how many escorts will there be?

- Will there be any selection by riding ability, or will there be mixed abilities with novice and experienced riders grouped together?

- What type of weather conditions are you likely to encounter? Will you still ride in extremes (heat, cold, rain, etc.)?

- What happens at night? Where do you stay? Where do the horses stay?

Riding holidays can be exciting, challenging and a wonderful experience. Procedures and standards may be very different from those you have experienced in the UK. Take your riding hat with you – you may not be offered one abroad! **LEFT** Beach riding in Jamaica.

- What provision is there for the care of the horses and their tacking up etc?

- What provision is made for a horse going lame during the holiday or a rider having an accident?

Riding holidays can be tremendous fun and can further your riding ability more quickly in one or two weeks than a once-a-week ride at a riding school can ever do. Riding holidays are probably most enjoyable if taken with a friend. If you travel alone, though, it is highly likely that you will meet like-minded people with whom you can share your experiences.

As with any speciality holiday, planning and preparation are essential and it is in your best interests to ensure that those involved in organising your holiday hold appropriate credentials for whatever they are offering. It is easy to be wise in hindsight after some mishap has occurred due to poor management.

Riding other people's horses

Sooner or later someone will offer you a horse to ride, and once you have achieved a level of competence in your riding this may be a great opportunity for extra riding.

Let us consider the advantages and disadvantages of such an offer and how you should deal with it so that everyone benefits.

Owners may offer you a ride because:

- They have a genuine desire for you to share the joy of riding their much-loved horse.

- They believe that their horse is nicer than anything else you might ever have ridden in the riding school.

- They do not have time to ride their horse very often and would like it to be exercised more regularly.

- The horse (because it lacks consistent work and attention) is a bit unruly and they hope that more frequent exercise will help to improve the situation.

- The horse has not been ridden for weeks or even months and their conscience will be eased if someone else takes some of the responsibility to ride the horse.

Any or some of these permutations may be behind the offer.

You must consider the following before committing yourself to ride a strange horse:

- The horse may never have been ridden by a relatively inexperienced rider and may well be used only to his owner. In fact, some privately owned horses can be quite disconcerted by being ridden by someone lacking confidence or competence and may react adversely purely through confusion. Riding-school horses, on the other hand, are well acquainted with being ridden by lots of different riders of all standards, and as a result school horses are well practised in 'looking after' a rider who is quite novicey.

■ It is unlikely that the horse will be presented to you tacked up and ready to ride (as probably happens in the riding school). You may be required to brush the horse and prepare him to ride, and then tack him up yourself. (See the section later in this chapter on caring for your horse.)

■ You will be solely responsible for mounting, checking your stirrups and girth and then setting forth on your ride. You must consider whether the owner will be there, either to help you before you start riding or to go with you when you ride.

■ Where will you ride this horse? Will it be in an enclosed arena (which you are used to) or will it be out in countryside which is unfamiliar to you?

■ Is the owner completely aware of how much experience you have had? Be totally honest with them about how long you have been riding, whether you can walk, trot and canter, and what your confidence level is.

Riding someone else's horse independently can bring untold joys and satisfaction, but do be aware of the possible shortcomings of such a venture. Then go and enjoy yourself.

Learning to look after a horse

If you are becoming a truly 'horse-mad person' then riding itself will not be sufficient and you will want to learn more about horses and stable management. Whether your riding school offers lessons in horsemastership other than riding is individual to each establishment, but broadening your knowledge of horses can be a very interesting and supporting part of the riding experience. In learning to handle, care for and manage your horse, as well as improving your riding skills, you will become an all-round horseman, which will enhance your relationship with horses.

Picking out the feet into a skip.

Knowledge of the following subjects would certainly be useful to you as a novice rider:

■ Basic handling. Moving around the horse safely. Putting on a headcollar. Tying up the horse.

■ Leading the horse in a headcollar. Turning the horse safely in hand. Standing the horse up, in hand.

■ Tacking up. Putting on a saddle and bridle. Fitting a headcollar over a bridle and tying up the horse safely.

■ Untacking. Removing the tack and replacing the horse's headcollar.

■ Handling the tack correctly and safely. Carrying and storing the tack.

■ Basic care of the tack.

Feeding your horse – tipping the feed into a fixed manger.

- Picking up the horse's feet, and picking them out.

- Turning the horse out into the field.

- Knowing the correct way to approach and catch a horse in the field, and how to bring him in.

- Grooming the horse before riding so that his tack will be comfortable.

- Understanding the basics of how to recognise a happy horse, an angry horse, a nervous horse, a tired horse and a horse that is not feeling well.

If your school doesn't teach these things, you can read up on them in any good book on horse care (*The BHS Complete Manual of Stable Management* would be a good place to start); then you will need to put your new-found knowledge into practice, initially with someone competent to guide and assist you.

chapter 10

Jumping

Many aspiring riders associate competence with the ability to jump. In running a commercial riding school for nearly twenty years it almost became a standing joke that when new riders came to the establishment and were asked about how much riding they had done, the competent people always were very modest and underestimated their ability, while the novice riders announced that they could canter and jump!

Learning to jump should be a natural and interesting progression from the work covered in the early chapters of this book. It can be introduced at any stage when:

- You have security in your basic position in walk, trot and canter.

- You can confidently move from one gait to another under your own initiative and control.

- You can easily vary your position from basic position to jumping position and back again.

- You can work without your stirrups in walk, trot and preferably canter.

- You have basic control in open order in walk, trot and preferably canter.

- Your position is sufficiently secure that you are never dependent on the reins for balance.

The rider's position over a jump

We have already covered the 'jumping position' (also known as the half-seat, light-seat, or poised position) on page 89, so we can now begin to think of using that position in relation to learning to jump.

When the horse jumps he gathers himself, transfers more weight onto his hind legs at the point of take-off, then springs into the air; on landing, his weight is taken onto his front legs before he re-takes his weight evenly over all four legs in the departure. The adaptation in the rider's position is purely to

This sequence shows the way in which the horse gathers himself to push himself into the air over the jump, and then lands with all his weight on his front feet, before bringing his hind legs under him to carry on forward away from the fence.

accommodate the changing phases of the horse's jump, and to enable the rider to maintain the best possible balance and harmony with the horse while jumping. It is important that the rider does not impede the horse so that he (the horse) can jump the fence with the minimum effort.

If we consider the jumping position with regard to jumping:

- As your depth and security improves you will tend to ride with a longer stirrup length in your basic riding position. For jumping, there will be an increasing need to shorten the stirrups to adopt a comfortable jumping position – probably one or two holes to start with, but your instructor should advise you individually.

- Your weight is distributed partly through your seat and partly through the lower leg and into the heels.

- You will need to shorten your reins.

- Your upper body inclines slightly forward, allowing the seat to slide more to the back of the saddle. This in turn closes the angles between the upper body and the thigh, and the thigh and the lower leg. These closed angles act as springs, giving the position the flexibility that allows riders to follow the horse's changing movement.

- You will learn to control your body movement as you develop your jumping ability. If you watch show-jumping riders you will see that they vary a little in their own particular style over a fence (some more forward, some more upright); the overall requirement of the jumping rider is that he must be in balance and harmony with the horse at all times.

As with all aspects of your riding, time and practice will build competence and confidence.

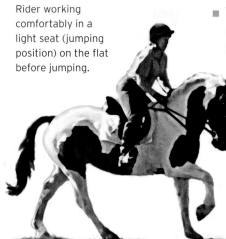

Rider working comfortably in a light seat (jumping position) on the flat before jumping.

Polework

Poles are used extensively as a preparation to jumping. We have already discussed their use as a way of providing interest and variation within lessons. Now we will look at how they can be utilised when teaching the novice rider to jump.

The natural two-beat sequence of the trot lends itself readily to work over poles. Trot is also a gait that can be used for jumping small fences, and the introduction of a small jump from a trot approach makes an easy first jumping exercise for novice riders.

Riding towards one (or more poles) requires:

- A well-planned corner and line of approach, aimed at the centre and coming at right angles to the pole(s).
- Riding the line with a regular rhythm and maintaining the same speed in the pace. The line of approach and departure are of great importance.

The gait going away from the fence may be the same as the approach or it may be in a faster gait – i.e. approach in trot; land and depart in canter.

If several poles are used they will be set at a distance of approximately 4ft 6ins (1.4m) apart – the distance will be set by your instructor and is a little dependent on the horses used in the lesson.

As a preparation for jumping you should be doing some of the following exercises:

- Riding to a single pole on the threequarter line, taking jumping position in the approach.
- Riding lines of three or four poles in different positions in the school, in jumping position.
- Practising riding to and away from lines of poles independently of other riders.
- Moving easily into jumping position and out of it again in all three gaits.

If you are working as a group over poles then riders should be at least four horse's lengths apart, and you should be advised that if a pole is knocked out of alignment you should circle away until it has been replaced.

You should never be in a position where, if an incident happens in front of you involving a pole (or later a jump), you are not in sufficient control to circle away, and therefore avoid compounding the problem.

First jump

It is a point of debate whether, as a novice rider, you should jump your first fence from a line of trotting poles or perhaps a single placing pole, or simply approach a plain single obstacle without a pole (or poles) in front. I can argue for both options, but, for me, there should never be only one way. There are many variables which must be considered:

- The horse and his way of jumping (a novice rider should always be mounted

Early jumping lessons. Using a placing pole to a small cross-pole.

on a sensible, smooth horse who is generous and willing in his desire to jump).

- The rider's confidence (some riders find a row of poles more daunting than a single fence).

- The facilities and time available.

The first jump can be taken from trot or canter, but if all the preparatory work has been done using trotting poles, the natural progression is to place one small jump approximately 9ft (2.9m) from the last trotting pole.

The first jump will either be a cross-pole, or a small upright or vertical fence.

Jumping a small vertical fence. In all these photos the rider is on the right lines for developing the correct jumping position but needs to establish greater depth and relaxation.

A class jumping lesson. Here one rider jumps while the other members of the class stand in a safe position and watch the proceedings

A cross-pole tends to look smaller (at the centre of the cross) and is an inviting fence which leads the horse and rider into the central point to jump at the lowest height. An upright fence, however, may be just as small, and may be slightly easier for the horse because the whole fence is the same height and he does not have to aim for the narrow point in the centre. In general, most instructors would choose a cross-pole as the first jump.

You should approach the poles in the way you have been practising, taking jumping position in the approach. The horse should smoothly negotiate the trotting pole(s) and then make a small jump over the fence taking a few strides in canter on landing. Your balance should be good enough to follow the horse's movement over this small jump, fluently in your jumping position. On landing, the basic riding position is re-taken as soon as possible to control the departure.

The single fence should be repeated frequently until you feel very confident about negotiating it. There is no substitute for practice, and repetition of this simple jump exercise is important.

If you are in any doubt about your ability to stay in balance over the fence, your instructor should encourage you to hold the horse's mane a little in front of the withers, about a third of the way up the horse's neck. This is preferable to having a neck-strap (a simple strap placed around the horse's neck), which tends to make you hold on too low down or too far back with your hands, neither of which will improve your balance and position over a jump.

When you can confidently approach the single fence on a good line and in control, and can jump the fence in a good balance, then it is time to negotiate two jumps. The easiest way to do this is to have one jump on one side of the school, and a second, single fence on the other. The aim is then to link the two fences together. You will then have to work on:

- Your line of approach to the first fence, and when to take jumping position.

- The line of departure from the first fence, the line around the top of the school, controlling the pace, your position and your line to the second fence.

- Your line of approach to the second fence and your position in the approach.

- Your departure from the second fence, controlling the pace, and your intended route thereafter.

Subsequent single fences can be positioned around the school to develop your control and balance. You can circle away from a fence at any time if you are not in sufficient balance or control to take the jump.

Once you are confident about your control and balance over single fences then the development of several fences linked together (a jumping grid) can be considered.

Grids

A grid is something that will probably become quite familiar to you as your jumping lessons progress. Jumping grids can serve a number of purposes, some of which are related to the training of horses (but this is outside the remit of this book). We will consider here the uses of grids to develop the skill of the rider and look at one or two simple grids which you may encounter in your lessons.

Grid work should be an easy progression from your first experience of jumping single fences. You should find that:

- It links one or more jumps together with one or two strides between each 'element' or jump.

- The strides and distances are measured so that you will know exactly where the horse will take off for each fence, enabling you to follow the movement easily.

- The grid can be systematically built up in height and difficulty to suit a range of abilities of rider in a group.

- Repetition of the same exercise helps to develop skill and confidence.

In the early stages of jumping grids the approach is likely to be in trot. It is also possible that there will be a placing pole to regulate the point of take-off (see diagram).
    The approach, jump and departure will be identical to your first jump exercise (see page 111). The departure from the jump will be in canter.
    The second element of the grid will be put in place when all riders in the group can negotiate the first element with ease. The second element will be set at either one 'non-jumping stride' (18ft/5.4m) or two 'non-jumping strides'

A simple grid exercise with a trot approach and three elements (jumps) to negotiate, landing and going away in canter.

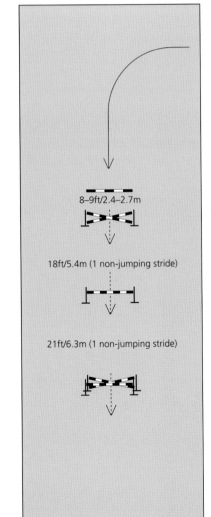

8–9ft/2.4–2.7m

18ft/5.4m (1 non-jumping stride)

21ft/6.3m (1 non-jumping stride)

NON-JUMPING STRIDES

A non-jumping stride is a stride which does not involve any part of a jump. For example, if a horse jumps a fence, lands, takes one or two strides between that fence and a second one, then takes off for the second fence, the non-jumping strides are strides between the fences. (Much later on you will learn that you can influence these non-jumping strides to shorten or lengthen the horse's stride between jumps.)

(28–30ft/8.4–9m). The first fence is likely to be a cross-pole; the second fence could be a small vertical or a small ascending spread fence (two rails to make a broader fence, with the front rail lower than the back rail).

When you can negotiate the two elements of the grid confidently then a third jump can be introduced. The third jump (element) can again be put at one or two non-jumping strides from the second. Because the horse has both taken off (for fence two) and landed to move to the next fence in canter the distance set will be slightly longer than the distance between fences one and two (for one stride it would be about 21ft/6.3m, for two strides it would be 30–33ft/9–9.9m).

The third fence could be a small upright or an ascending spread fence.

Jumping a grid teaches you to develop more efficiency in your jumping position. As the jumps come together in a sequence you must learn to adopt jumping position in the approach to fence one, then follow the movement over each fence with a developing ability to stay in balance through the whole grid. As you feel the horse's movement through the grid and the way he gathers himself to jump each jump, it should become increasingly easy to move in harmony with him as he flows down the line of jumps. Ideally the horse you ride should be calm and regular in the way he jumps the grid; he should not hurry, getting faster and faster either down the line of jumps or in the approach.

Jumping grids can be great fun and should develop your confidence and 'feel' in jumping. Grids also prepare you for jumping 'combination' fences , i.e. doubles and trebles, which, if you progress with your riding, you will encounter in jumping courses and eventually perhaps in competition, if you decide to follow that option.

Jumping outdoors

Jumping outdoors, like riding outdoors, is like the difference between swimming in a pool and swimming in the sea. If your ability and confidence are developing, then jumping outside can be a very natural progression, offering variety and new challenges.

Jumping on a surface in an outdoor arena is very similar to jumping in an indoor school, but jumping in a field on grass gives you a very different feeling. Grass has a less consistent surface than an arena and is not so level, and you

Cross-country instruction – learning to jump fixed natural-type obstacles.

will therefore need to accept that you may feel less secure. You may need to exert greater control over the horse in both pace and direction (there are no walls to help influence the horse and therefore the control). Jumping outside is great fun, though, and if a class jumping lesson is well organised by your instructor and the obstacles used are well chosen and explained then you should enjoy the experience.

It would be sensible for your first experience of jumping outside to be over some simple, single, show-jump type fences, as these are the types of jump you have become competent over in the school. The next big step is to think about cross-country jumping.

Jumping natural obstacles

We have talked about riding outside and the options for riding on bridlepaths, forestry commission land and moorland. In these sorts of environment it is easy to develop walk, trot and canter confidently. If your position is more secure and versatile, which should be the case if you have practised both the basic position and the jumping position in the circumstances described, then being able to 'raise the pace' in the country should, in due course, come fairly naturally.

Riding in the countryside and being able to jump any small obstacle which is in the way, can be fun and challenging. Whether it is a small log, a little ditch to pop over or a stream to splash through, your main aim should be to stay in balance with the horse, follow his movement and stay in a position where you feel secure and in control.

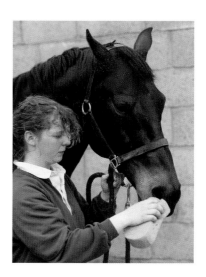

chapter **11**

A horse of your own?

The pros and cons

Let's assume that you are now thoroughly 'horse mad', 'bitten by the bug' and confined to eternal bankruptcy, thanks to horses! I will try and put the case very simply for and against having a horse of your own – then the decision must be yours and yours alone. There will always be people 'in the know' about horses, who will 'expertly' advise you on what you should do, which horse you should buy and then what you should do with it. Do remember that often those 'advising' you may have a hidden agenda for wanting you to buy this or that horse (they may be trying to sell it, want you to keep it in their yard or want to teach you on it). Inexperienced, newly 'horse mad' people are very vulnerable to the plausible 'horse expert' who is anxious to help you part with your cash. Be very careful about who you take advice from.

Advantages of owning a horse

- It will give you the opportunity to ride whenever you want, for as long as you want and wherever you want.

- You can develop a rapport and relationship with your horse and your riding skills should develop as a result.

- You may enjoy looking after a horse and caring for his needs.

- The horse is ridden exclusively by you and learns to 'go' for you in the way you want him to.

- You may adore the feeling of 'ownership'.

- It may fulfil a dream.

Disadvantages of owning a horse

- You will have to consider the cost implications. The initial purchase will involve capital outlay from around £2,000 to £8,000 (for a well-schooled,

Owning your own horse or pony should give you a wonderful friend from whom you will gain hours of pleasure both riding and caring for him.

calm, obedient, easy mannered horse, which would be suitable for a first-time horse owner).

- Keeping the horse will involve a weekly cost (either you keep him at home, which requires facilities, or you keep him at livery – board him at a stables where you pay someone else to look after him. For the latter, depending on the extent of the service, the cost may be from £20 for DIY (do-it-yourself) to £120 per week for full livery).

- The horse will need shoeing regularly (every four to six weeks) at a cost of around £50 for a set of shoes . He will need some annual veterinary care (e.g. inoculations) and may need veterinary attention from time to time.

- There are other peripheral costs, such as equipment, tuition, insurance, competition entries, transport, etc. I am afraid the list is never-ending.

- Horses need 365-day care, and you must make the necessary arrangements to cater for his needs whenever you go away on holiday, take a weekend break, are ill, or at any time when you just can't find the energy or enthusiasm to go and visit him.

- Being a horse owner involves responsibility, and if there are any problems (in, say, riding, feeding or welfare) then you must take decisions for your horse in his best interests. If you do not feel you have sufficient knowledge or experience to do that then you will have to seek professional advice (perhaps from your riding instructor at the school where you learned), but this is likely to involve a fee (just as hiring the services of a lawyer, dentist or builder). Professional advice costs money; there will be plenty of 'amateurs' willing to share their knowledge, but beware, because it may not always be helpful or correct.

Owning a horse often goes hand in hand with owning a dog. The two are usually very compatible. The three of you can have lots of fun!

If I have not put you off completely then do seek sound advice before taking this huge step.

Leasing or loaning a horse

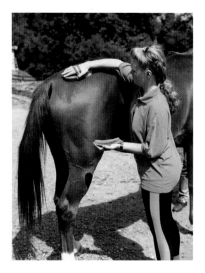

Caring for your horse includes giving him a good groom - all part of the pleasure of owning a horse.

Leasing or loaning a horse may seem like the ideal situation to enable you to become the 'owner' of a horse without the capital outlay, but again I would voice very great caution.

There are satisfactory lease or loan arrangements, but on the whole they are a minefield of potential problems. If you decide to follow this route be very sure that both parties are absolutely sure of what arrangement is in place. It is sensible to get an agreement formally drawn up by a solicitor and have both parties sign their acceptance – otherwise these amicable arrangements can so easily end in tears.

Look into the lease/loan terms and if possible adapt them to suit your own situation. Consider some of the following points:

■ Is there any cost involved (annual fee)?

■ Who pays for any unforeseen veterinary charges?

■ What notice is given of the owner wanting the horse back?

■ What happens if the horse improves radically with the new rider (becomes much more valuable)? Who benefits?

■ What happens if the horse suffers a chronic lameness which affects its continuing use as a riding horse?

■ What happens if you do not get on with the horse?

Some leading horse magazines (*Horse and Hound*, for example) carry advertisements for loan and lease arrangements. Do go down that road if you want to, but with great caution.

chapter 12

What next?

Tests of competence

British Horse Society-Approved riding schools often run tests of competence called **Progressive Riding Tests**. These tests can give you a 'bench mark' as to your progress.

Set at **six** different levels (number 1 being the most basic, and number 6 the most demanding) they are aimed at the weekly rider and can be worked on in your normal weekly riding lessons. They cover both riding competence and basic horse care and stable management.

Full information and syllabi for the tests can be obtained from the BHS (whose address is listed at the back of this book) or ask your riding school about them.

Joining a riding club

If you want to become involved with like-minded horse lovers then a riding club can provide an ideal environment.

You do not necessarily need to own your own horse, and membership can be rewarding in many ways. You will meet new friends, and you can attend the events organised by the club, such as competitions, training sessions, social get-togethers or visits to lecture-demonstrations in the locality. If you finally become a horse owner then obviously you will be able to take part in competitions if you so choose.

Riding clubs may be organised 'in house' by the riding school (in which case you may be able to hire a horse to take part in their competitions), or they may be run under the 'British Riding Clubs' banner and affiliated to the British Horse Society. A British Riding Club will always welcome non-riding members as there is much 'behind-the-scenes' organisation for which non-riders can volunteer.

Information about British Riding Clubs can be obtained from the Riding Club's office (their address can be found at the back of this book).

Pleasure rides

Pleasure rides can be a wonderful way of enjoying beautiful countryside. Pleasure rides are sometimes organised by local Riding Clubs/Pony Clubs or by private individuals to provide a designated route over a certain distance, for the leisure rider.

Pleasure rides usually vary from between five and fifteen miles, and most horses and riders thoroughly enjoy the chance to ride with other horsey folk and to spend time enjoying the partnership with their horse. Look out for these pleasure rides in the local press. Check who is organising the ride, and, if possible, take advice from those who have done the ride before as to its suitability for more novice riders.

Unaffiliated competitions

If and when you take the plunge to buy your own horse, you may choose to start competing. Unaffiliated shows run throughout the summer, and some centres now run classes throughout the winter months as well. Whether you choose to start your competitive career with a small 'clear round' jumping class or a straightforward dressage test is your choice. Unaffiliated competitions generally offer smaller jumping tests and more simple dressage tests, and are often informally organised with a lot of voluntary labour. Affiliated classes, on the other hand, are organised under stringent and consistent guidelines so that the classes will be the same in terms of requirements and method of judging, wherever they are held.

Unaffiliated competitions may be run in your area by:

■ Competition centres.

Clear-round jumping or local riding club competitions are usually easily accessible. Cross-country rides or eventing can be something to aim for.

Jumping natural obstacles that you meet while hacking can be fun and teach your horse to be versatile.

- Riding Club or Pony Club (often non-members are welcome and these shows are often referred to as 'open shows').

- An organising committee to raise funds for local charities.

These competitions will probably be advertised in your local tack store or feed merchant, and horse people in your community, such as your instructor or farrier, will often know where to get advice and a schedule.

Riding holidays

These have already been discussed in Chapter 9.

Falling off

I cannot write a book on learning to ride without mentioning 'falling off' or parting company with your horse in an unplanned way!

If, say, you run up a flight of stairs often enough, sooner or later you will find it very easy to do. By running daily you encourage the body to build the appropriate muscles and make the heart and lungs work more efficiently. Also, if you go up and down those stairs often enough, sooner or later you will slip (and not quite regain your balance) and, irrespective of how often you have climbed those stairs, you will fall. Riding horses is like that. It does not matter how good your instructor is, how naturally you have taken to riding and how obedient your horse is, you are likely to fall off at some time. Falling off is a 'very small' part of riding. No one can, or ever should, guarantee that you will never fall off. In the event of any type of fall (whether it happens slowly or much faster as in racing) it is rare and bad luck if you do yourself any lasting harm. Never dwell on 'what might happen' – it then rarely does! Aim for developing as much relaxation, depth in your position and understanding for control as you can. In the eventuality of a fall occurring:

- Try to relax and curl up as you fall, keeping your head a little protected by the rest of your body and your arms tucked in. Avoid putting a hand out to break your fall or you may end up breaking your wrist.

- Injury will be minimal or non-existent if you are relaxed in your fall.

- Let go of the horse as you fall. Holding on may give you a nasty jolt through your arm and damage shoulder or neck.

- Do not be in a hurry to leap up from the ground. Lie still for a time until you have decided if and where you are in pain.

- In a school situation, assistance should be very swift, and your instructor should advise you on what to do, depending on how you feel and subject to assessment to be sure that there are no apparent problems.

- Remount again, as long as you have not experienced any pain as a result of the fall or had a bang on the head. Otherwise do not attempt to continue to ride for the rest of the session. Your instructor should advise you on whether to remount or not.

- Continue your riding and avoid dwelling on the experience unnecessarily. Ride a horse in which you have high confidence and attempt the exercise where the problem arose, again. Your instructor should guide the work and support you to ensure that the problem (if avoidable) does not arise again.

Most riders come to accept falling off as an 'occupational hazard'. Having said that, if you are well taught, on well-trained horses in a safe environment, falling off should be a very rare occurrence.

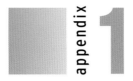

About The British Horse Society

The British Horse Society is a charity to promote the welfare, care and use of the horse and pony; to develop correct training of the horse; to encourage horsemastership and the improvement of horse management and breeding; and to represent all equine interests.

The Society is internationally recognised as the premier equestrian riding, training and examination organisation in the United Kingdom, and operates an Approvals scheme for all types of equestrian establishment. It incorporates some 390 Riding Clubs and works closely with the Pony Club. The Society is also the national governing body for recreational riding and fully supports the independent sporting disciplines within the British Equestrian Federation.

The BHS plays a major role in equine welfare, safety, provision of access to the countryside, and protection of riding and driving Rights of Way. It represents riders to Government and to the EU in Brussels in all matters, especially those concerning taxation, rates, planning and the law.

Membership benefits include £5 million public liability insurance, personal accident insurance, a yearbook, magazines, special facilities and discounts at BHS functions, and access to BHS advice and support.

The BHS is the biggest membership organisation in the United Kingdom dedicated to the welfare of the horse, its training and development. With an impressive membership of around 59,000 and approximately 40,000 Riding Club members, it is the largest organisation within the British Equestrian Federation.

By joining the Society you are helping all who ride. For further information and membership details contact the Society at the address opposite.

Useful addresses

British Horse Society
Stoneleigh Deer Park
Kenilworth
Warwickshire
CV8 2XZ
tel: 08701 202244
or   01926 707700
fax: 01926 707800
website: www.bhs.org.uk
email: enquiry@bhs.org.uk

BHS Examinations Department
(address as above)
tel: 01926 707784
fax: 01926 707800
email: exams@bhs.org.uk

BHS Training Department
(address as above)
tel: 01926 707822
     01926 707821
email: training@bhs.org.uk

**BHS Riding Schools/Approvals
   Department**
(address as above)
tel: 01926 707795
fax: 01926 707796
email: Riding.Schools@bhs.org.uk

BHS Bookshop
(address as above)
tel: 08701 201918
     01926 707762
website: www.britishhorse.com

British Riding Clubs Department
(address as above)
tel: 01926 707769
fax: 01926 707764
email: s.long@bhs.org.uk

Further reading

The following and other BHS publications are available from the BHS Bookshop and from tackshops and booksellers.

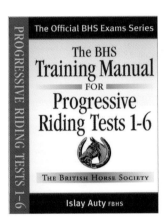

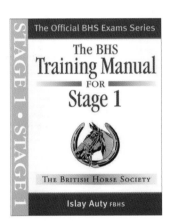

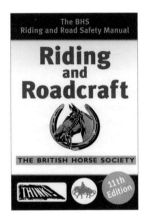

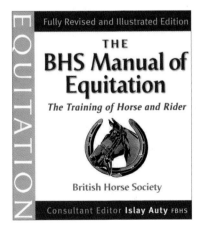

Index

Note: Page numbers in **bold** type indicate figures or photographs in the text